Notes On The Book Of Nehemiah

Second Edition

by

H.A. Ironside

www.solidchristianbooks.com

Contents

Preface To The Second Edition 3

Prefatory Note 4

Introduction..5

Chapter I An Exercised Man...................................8

Chapter II The Failed Testimony.............................11

Chapter III The Gates of Jerusalem 18

Chapter IV Soldier-Servants.................................41

Chapter V Internal Strife...................................47

Chapter VI Plots And Snares.................................53

Chapter VII Restoring Order.................................60

Chapter VIII The Great Bible-Reading 68

Chapter IX The Word And Prayer 74

Chapter X The New Start 79

Chapter XI A Willing People.................................86

Chapter XII The Dedication Of The Wall 90

Chapter XIII Vigilance *Versus* Declension 95

Preface To The Second Edition

In going over these pages again after the lapse of nearly twelve years I feel more than ever the importance of the truths on which they insist. The need for holy separation from the world and worldly Christianity is more evident with each passing day, as the dispensation nears its close. On the other hand the need of increasing largeness of heart toward God's beloved people struggling against the evil and crying for light and for help becomes more manifest. To all such I send forth this little book again on its mission of love.

H. A. Ironside

June, 1925

Prefatory Note

The little book now before the reader has been in contemplation ever since its companion-exposition, "Notes on the Book of Ezra," was published. If read in connection with that work and also the writer's "Notes on Esther" (the three issued separately, also in one volume), and the "Notes on Haggai, Zechariah, and Malachi" in the volume on "The Minor Prophets," a connection will be traced throughout.

As heretofore, no attempt has been made to write for scholars or to produce a literary work. But in the simplest way I have sought to emphasize important truths that are being neglected in many places where they need to be pressed more insistently than ever.

The Lord watch over all for His name's sake.

H. A. Ironside

Nov. 1913

Introduction

In the book of Ezra, we see a remnant people gathered back to the place where the Lord had set His name, after a long period of bondage and exile in Babylon, the centre of the false religious system of that day. Nehemiah pursues the further history of this company for some years afterwards, but is especially devoted to the work of guarding the place of privilege, as indicated in the large space given to the narration of events in connection with the building of the wall of Jerusalem. This was a wall both of protection and exclusion, and doubtless speaks to us to-day of principles which may easily be abused where self-judgment and spirituality are lacking, but which are nevertheless of supreme importance if any scriptural testimony is to be maintained in a day of declension. It is considered a mark of liberality and brotherly kindness with many, to declaim against all exclusive-ness on the part of believers in the Lord Jesus Christ. But it is to be feared numbers object to a term they neither understand nor see the reason for.

A word in the book of Deuteronomy might help as to this. In chapter 22:8 we read: "When thou buildest a new house, then thou shalt make a battlement for thy roof, that thou bring not blood upon thy house if any man fall from thence." The battlement surrounding the flat roof of the Israelite's dwelling conveys much the same thought as the wall enclosing Jerusalem. The roof was to the oriental the place of communion and retirement (1 Sam. 9:25; Prov. 21:9), of prayer (Acts 10:9), and of testimony (Matt. 10:27). It was commonly used very much as both the parlor and the study of the occidental. There the family would commune together, and there they would entertain friends. But if there were no protecting wall about this favored place, it would be one of danger to the young and to any inclined to be careless. Therefore the divine instruction that a battlement be built to completely surround the house-top; otherwise the owner of the house was held responsible if any one fell from thence, and so was slain.

The house-top is a fitting picture of assembly privilege. For, as gathered to the name of the Lord Jesus, believers are in the place of retirement from the distracting things of the world, of communion with the Father and the Son, and with one another, in the Spirit's power, and this is likewise the place of prayer and of testimony. But hallowed as such a place is, there are always the young in Christ and those weak in the faith to be considered. Pre-eminently for their sakes it is imperative that the wall of separation (not only from the world, but from worldly Christianity) be maintained, otherwise many of these little ones will fall from this hallowed sphere of privilege into which grace has brought them.

And here I desire to quote the words of a brother beloved, written in a private letter some time since, but which I feel are of value for all believers desiring so to walk as to please God, not only individually, but in corporate testimony: "By some an attempt is being made to pull down the barriers of truth and make us give up what we have. If the younger men among us, who are soon to take the lead, if the Lord tarry yet a while, are not true in practice to the truth, not only of the gospel but also of the Church of God, the truth itself will slip away from them. As I see the developments all around, I burn with jealousy for the truth we have. It makes us, in its practice, a people rejected by all, but who have the bread that *all need.* If we keep separated from every movement which leaves out what hurts in the truth; if we just live out in practice what the truth is, we will remain no doubt a small, unpopular people, but we will be to the end God's vessel of truth to His whole Church on earth; and that will be ten thousand times better throughout eternity than to have been on popular lines for greater access to men.

"Our assemblies, if kept truly pure, are little fortresses for the defence and sallying out of truth. Let us build them up strong, solid and faithful... Principles of independency *annul the constitution* of the Church of God as laid down in Ephesians, and make it impossible for us therefore to carry out its by-laws, as I may call them, given us in Corinthians."[1]

These are sound and seasonable words, and form a fitting introduction to the special lines of divine truth emphasized in this instructive portion of the word of God, the book of Nehemiah.

The years that have passed since they were written have witnessed the rapid development of apostasy in the form of Modernism, making it more imperative than ever that real believers should walk in separation from those who deny every fundamental truth of Scripture.

Chapter I An Exercised Man

In the twentieth year of Artaxerxes, king of Persia, his cup-bearer, Nehemiah, the son of Hachaliah, was in deep exercise of soul concerning the condition of the re-gathered remnant, whose history we have been studying, as related by Ezra the Scribe.[2] Nehemiah means *comfort* or *consolation of Jehovah,* and he is one whose name expresses his character, as is so often the case in Scripture, when names were not given by any means so carelessly as now. Like Paul, he was to comfort others with the comfort wherewith he himself was comforted of God (2 Cor. 1:4). This is a weighty principle in God's ways with His servants. Many a saint is permitted to go through deep waters, to pass through severe trial both of body and mind, not only for his own profit, but that he may be the better fitted to be a channel of blessing to his brethren when cast down and in distress. Happy is the saint who is thus subject to the will of God and enabled to be His agent in consoling his discouraged fellows and restoring them, through a ministry received in times of sorrow, when they are backslidden and disheartened.

The station of Nehemiah was one of worldly-prosperity. It is true he was a servant; probably a bondman, but so were all his people; and he dwelt in a royal palace, and seems to have been a favorite with the king. But, like Moses, his heart was with his lowly brethren, and his spirit was zealous for the testimony of the Lord.

To him, Hanani, one of his brethren, and other Jews came, whom he questioned closely concerning the remnant who had gone up to Jerusalem. The report was not encouraging. They replied: "The remnant that are left of the captivity there in the province are in great affliction and reproach; the wall of Jerusalem also is broken down, and the gates thereof are burned with fire" (ver. 3). That Hanani felt this keenly there can be no doubt, but that he, or his companions were before God about it, as was Nehemiah, seems scarcely probable. It is one thing to shake the head and sigh over the vicissitudes of the congregation of the Lord, it is quite another to look up to Him to give deliverance, and to put His truth and testimony above every other interest. This latter Nehemiah did.

His brethren's unhappy report caused him deepest searching of heart and contrition of spirit, so that he gave himself to fasting and prayer with many tears; for, like Paul in a brighter dispensation, he knew much of what it was to weep over the failures of the people of God. To Him who had forsaken His city and given His people up to captivity, but who had granted a little reviving in their bondage, Nehemiah turned in prayer. He uses the same title so frequently found in the record of Ezra, "the God of heaven." This indicated the removal of God's throne from earth to heaven. In deepest humiliation he joins with Ezra and Daniel in confessing his sin and the sin of his people. "We have sinned," he cries; and again, "Both I and my father's house have sinned;" and once more, "We have dealt very corruptly." Genuine confession like this reaches the ear of God. It indicates a soul able to look at matters from God's standpoint. Nehemiah is no carping critic, no self-satisfied Pharisaic looker-on upon the failure of others. "I thank Thee that I am not as other men" would never come from his lips. Instead, he bows his head in common confession with his brethren, and brokenly cries, "We have sinned."

But he is a man of faith as well as a man of prayer, and so he at once proceeds to remind God, as it were, of His own word; how He had declared in Lev. 26:40-45 and Deut. 4:23; 30:1-6 that even though He might scatter His people because of their transgression, yet if in the stranger's land they would turn unto Him, keep His commandments, and do them, He would gather them again, though it were from the uttermost parts of the earth, and bring them back to the place He had chosen, "to set His name there." This promise Nehemiah pleads, and touchingly cries: "Now these are Thy servants and Thy people, whom Thou hast redeemed by Thy great power and by Thy strong hand. O Lord, I beseech Thee, let now Thine ear be attentive to the prayer of Thy servant, and to the prayer of Thy servants who desire to fear Thy name: and prosper, I pray Thee, Thy servant this day, and grant him mercy in the sight of this man" (vers. 10, 11). "This man" was none other than the great Arta-xerxes himself; but to Nehemiah he was just a man, and he desired that his heart might be controlled by God for the furtherance of His purpose of grace towards His people.

In other circumstances he could and did give honor to whom honor was due. But in the presence of the great King of kings this puissant monarch was but a man, and such is he in Nehemiah's reckoning. He had, in large measure, learned to put not his trust in princes, but to cease from man whose breath is in his nostrils. To the living God he looked; on His compassion and omnipotence he reckoned; and the sequel shows that he was not disappointed.

Chapter II The Failed Testimony

It pleased the God of heaven, in bringing about an answer to His servant's petition, to attract the attention of the Persian ruler to the grief-stricken face of Nehemiah. Kindly the monarch inquires after the cause of this change of countenance, for the son of Hachaliah had been wont to exhibit a cheerful mien, as became one whose confidence was in the Lord. "Why is thy countenance sad," asks the king, "seeing thou art not sick? This is nothing else but sorrow of heart." Fearful of his sovereign's displeasure, his cupbearer replies, "Let the king live forever: why should not my countenance be sad, when the city, the place of my father's sepulchres, lieth waste, and the gates thereof are consumed with fire?" (ver. 23). Nehemiah could not be indifferent to a matter of this kind. He was no misanthropical pessimist—rather indeed the very opposite—but he could not be unmoved by the terrible breakdown on the part of his loved people and the desolate condition of that city that should have been the glory of the whole earth.

But, observe, he did not stand aside and write pamphlets on the failure of his brethren or simply denounce them for their backslidings while doing nothing to help them reach a better state; nor did he wash his hands of the whole matter and conclude that because the failure had indeed come in, he was justified in giving up all concern about the testimony committed to Judah. Not at all. His was a grief deep and genuine; but it was one that led to exercise before God, and an earnest desire to be an instrument in the hand of the Lord for the establishment of the truth, and the recovery and encouragement of the feeble few who had broken down so sadly in the very place where Jehovah had set His name.

And so when the king inquired, "For what dost thou make request?" he did not answer till he had "prayed to the God of heaven." What an atmosphere of prayer surrounds this man! It is his constant resource throughout all his varied experiences. He walked with God because he talked with God. Now, assured of the Lord's mind, he made request for permission to visit the land of Judah and the city of Jerusalem, that he might "build it." This was morally very lovely. He desired to build, to edify. Any one with a small measure of discernment can stand off and either bewail or criticize the failures of others, but one must needs be in touch with God to be a true builder. Such an one was Paul, "a wise master-builder," and he, by the Spirit, directs that "all things be done unto edifying." "Knowledge," he tells us, "puffeth up, but love edifieth" (or, build-eth up). This is an all-important truth.

Many there are who entered on the path of separation with high hopes and fond expectations; eagerly they drank in the precious truths the Holy Spirit of God was making known in the place where He had liberty to work as He would. But to-day, alas, alas! many of these have turned away disheartened, and that because of breakdown on the part of brethren whom these others deem less clear of sight, less devoted and less intelligent than themselves. So they stand off and bewail the divided condition, the worldliness, the cold-heartedness that has come in among those who sought to walk together in separation from the prevailing apostasy. But to what end? Such a course profits neither those who so judge, nor those judged. Better, a thousand times better, to rise up in the spirit of Nehemiah, and throw oneself in the breach as a builder. The heart may be grieved and the countenance sad, but there will be a deep-toned joy in seeking thus to enlighten, instruct, and edify weaker brethren: endeavoring in the fear of God to keep the Spirit's unity in the bond of peace, and occupy saints with the blessed Gatherer Himself instead of the failure of those gathered.

Yes, as the days darken and the dispensation fast hastens to its close, it is men of the Nehemiah stamp who will be of real value to the people of God, and who shall thus save themselves and those who hear them.

In the presence of his consort, Artaxerxes gave the desired permission, stipulating a defined leave of absence, in which Nehemiah would be free to carry out the desire of his heart, and go to his brethren as a true prophet to speak words of exhortation, edification and encouragement (ver. 6). All that may be needed for the work of building is granted by the king, even as the King of kings, who is also head of His body, the Church, delights to supply His willing workers with all things that pertain to the ministry committed to them. And here we note that Ezra and Nehemiah were men of like mind in tracing every blessing to the good hand of God (ver. 8).

The intervening journey soon completed (for a burning love urged him on), Nehemiah crosses the river and presents the king's letters to the governors of the mixed Samaritan people, who had been settled in the land of the ten tribes since the days of Esar-haddon. At once we read of two men who are grieved and displeased; they were Sanballat the Horonite and Tobiah the Ammonite, called contemptuously, Tobiah the *servant.* When they heard of his arrival, "it grieved them exceedingly that there was come a man to seek the welfare of the children of Israel" (ver. 10). As these men caused Nehemiah much trouble and concern later on, it will be well to inquire here as to who or what they might represent, and to ask if any such adversaries are likely to be encountered to-day in connection with the defence of the "present truth."

Sanballat is called a Horonite, generally supposed to mean a native of Horonaim, a city of Moab. Of Tobiah's ancestry we are left in no doubt. We have therefore in these two foes representatives of those hostile races of whom it was written, "The Moabite and the Ammonite should not come into the congregation of God forever," as we are reminded later in chapter 13:1. The prohibition in Deut. 23:3-6 gives the reason for this: "An Ammonite or Moabite shall not enter into the congregation of the Lord; even to their tenth generation shall they not enter into the congregation of the Lord forever: because they met you not with bread and water in the way, when ye came forth out of Egypt; and because they hired against thee Balaam the son of Beor of Pethor of Mesopotamia, to curse thee. Nevertheless...the Lord thy God turned the curse into a blessing unto thee, because the Lord thy God loved thee. Thou shalt not seek their peace nor their prosperity all thy days forever."

Reading such a command, we naturally ask why such a doom upon Moab and Ammon for refusing aid to Israel when about to enter the land of promise? Why should it have been expected of them and not of others? The answer is very simple. There were ties of blood that gave Israel right to expect their assistance, but these ties were utterly repudiated. Moab and Ammon were the natural sons of Lot, but by his own daughters! They were really then "bastards, and not sons" (Heb. 12:8). They surely speak to us of those professing to be children of God, but not born of the Spirit. And so they ever, as born only of the flesh, persecuted the spiritual seed. They are the representatives of fleshly religion, of carnal profession, and as such they detest reality, and hate the truth that, "Except a man be

14

born again he cannot see the kingdom of God." They feel they have as much right to the ordinances of God, and as much liberty to participate in His service and worship as any; but they are only natural men with a veneer of religiousness, and such have ever been the bitterest opponents of what really honors Christ and glorifies God. They abound to-day as they have abounded all down the centuries, and their object is still, as ever, to corrupt if they can, and to destroy if they cannot corrupt. Leaving Sanballat and Tobiah for the present, gnashing their teeth in their rage and vexation, we follow Nehemiah to the city of God. Reaching Jerusalem, he rested three days. Then, conferring not with flesh and blood, but taking a few men with him, though telling none what God had put in his heart, he arose in the night and went out to view in silence the ruin that had come in. This night journey around the walls of the city is deeply pathetic. "Who that has any real care for the people of God has not known something of it? The nobles and rulers and all the people are wrapt in slumber, but this lonely man, whose heart God has touched, keeps his midnight vigil, and goes from gate to gate and tower to tower, noting with deepest sorrow and concern the breaches sin has made. "I went out by night," he says, "by the gate of the valley, even before the dragon well, and to the dung port, and viewed the walls of Jerusalem, which were broken down, and the gates thereof were consumed with fire. Then I went on to the gate of the fountain, and to the king's pool: but there was no place for the beast that was under me to pass. Then went I up in the night by the brook, and viewed the wall, and turned back and entered by the gate of the valley, and so returned" (vers. 13-15). It was no carping critic viewing with indifferent feelings the defencelessness of his brethren; but a man of purpose and prayer, beholding what stirred his soul to its depths, with the desire to build up what carnal ease and self-seeking had permitted to fall into ruin.

It was not till after this night view that he called the people, with their rulers and the priests of the Lord together, to give them cognizance of his mission. He does so most delicately. There are no reproaches, no Pharisaic and odious comparisons or contrasts, but he identifies himself fully with them and says: "Ye see the distress that we are in; how Jerusalem lieth waste, and the gates thereof are burned with fire: come, and let us build up the wall of Jerusalem, that we be no more a reproach" (ver. 17). Such an one is a God-sent and Spirit-qualified leader. He does not say, "You are in distress;" but "We are." He does not command, "Go, and build," but he entreats, "Let us build." He does not say, "You are a reproach," but he pleads, "Let us be no more a reproach." And then he tells of the good hand of his God upon him, and of the king's commission.

The people are aroused and encouraged, and cry at once, "Let us rise up and build;" and so they join hands with God's dear servant for the work he has planned. No doubt there was not the exercise of soul in all that conditions called for; but the work must be done nevertheless, and there will be more exercise as they go on.

And now we hear of Sanballat and Tobiah again; and with them a third adversary, Geshem the Arabian. This man is either an Edomite or an Ishmaelite, more probably the latter; but in either case he speaks of the flesh warring against the Spirit. Both Ishmael and Esau were types of the natural man—hence of the flesh—and were opposed to Isaac and Jacob, the seed of promise. Geshem is elsewhere in this book called Gashmu. When this unworthy trio hear of the work contemplated at the place of the Name, they indulge in sarcastic merriment. Nehemiah noted that, "They laughed us to scorn, and despised us, and said, What is this thing that ye do? will ye rebel against the king?" (ver. 19).

Heretofore the line of demarcation between the outwardly separated Israelites and these mixed nations had been almost obliterated; hence there was peace and quietness. But now a man has come who contemplates rearing afresh the wall of exclusion, and this is bitterly resented, though at first they attempt but to laugh down the determination of the remnant. To all their sneers Nehemiah calmly replies: "The God of heaven, He will prosper us; and therefore we His servants will arise and build: but ye have no portion, nor right, nor memorial, in Jerusalem!" (ver. 20). He has thrown down the gauntlet and declares his uncompromising attitude in a manner not to be misunderstood. Henceforth he will be hated as only those can hate who resent having their false religious claims made nothing of! The out-and-out worldling does not hate what is truly of God so bitterly as the Christless professor who has a name that he lives but is dead. Such an one cannot bear spiritual realities; for when confronted with them the hollowness of his profession is exposed, like Dagon when the ark of Jehovah was set down before it. This explains the bitterness with which these adversaries opposed the work of God going on at Jerusalem.

Chapter III The Gates of Jerusalem

The work at once began, and it is to be noted what a thoroughly individual thing it was. Nehemiah is the servant used to stir up the rest; but they *are* stirred up, and "To every man his work" is the motto that might well describe the busy scene. This chapter is like a page from the books of God's record of service, and will doubtless be opened at the judgment seat of Christ, when each will be rewarded for his own work—and some who shirked, alas, will then suffer loss. For both the workers and the shirkers are here mentioned, and here their names shall stand till the Lord Himself has pronounced His judgment upon all. Such records are deeply instructive, and deserve to be pondered with care that they may stir up our minds by way of remembrance.

In the New Jerusalem there are to be twelve gates (Rev. 21:12), and each several gate of one pearl; so that, look upon the city from whichever standpoint one may, he will be reminded of the precious truth that Christ "loved the Church, and gave Himself for it" (Eph. 5:25). He came from heaven as a merchantman seeking goodly pearls; and having found one pearl of great price, He bought it, at the cost of all that He had; "though He was rich, for our sakes He became poor," that we might be rich. And that heavenly city, of which Christ is the centre and the lamp for the display of God's glory, has "a wall great and high," speaking, as did the wall of the earthly city, of security and exclusion.

Jerusalem in Nehemiah's day seems to have had twelve gates also, though only ten are mentioned in this chapter: but in chapter 8:16 we read of "the gate of Ephraim," and in 12:39 of "the prison gate." The ten mentioned in the present portion remind us of the number that, it has been well said, sets forth responsibility towards God and man, of which the ten words in the law were the measure; while the twelve of the heavenly city (and note how many twelves there are in Rev. 21), as some have suggested, would set forth perfect administration, or governmental completeness, only to be known in the day that the kings of the earth bring the glory and the honor of the nations unto it.

I have thought there might be divine lessons for us in the names and order of these gates. That there is danger always of being fanciful, I realize. An insubject imagination is only "evil continually" (Gen. 6:5), in the things of the Lord as well as in all else, and one would therefore seek to avoid it. But, in looking at these gates, it is not so much my thought to seek to give the interpretation of them as to make a practical application of truth which, I am convinced, is much needed in this Laodicean day. We shall therefore take them in their order, as we go through the chapter, noting likewise the interesting and instructive points brought out in connection with service as we go from port to port. We begin, then, with

The Sheep Gate,

of which we read in the first verse: "Eliashib the high priest rose up with his brethren the priests, and they builded the sheep gate; they sanctified it, and set up the doors of it; even unto the tower of Meah they sanctified it, unto the tower of Hananeel."

This was priestly work indeed, for through this gate the beasts were led whose death and blood-shedding were to picture the one Offering of the ninth of Hebrews. They pointed on to the perfect sacrifice of that unnamed One of Isaiah 53, who was "led as a lamb to the slaughter, and

19

as a sheep before her shearers is dumb, so He openeth not His mouth."

Thankful we are that for us it is not necessary to ask, as did the eunuch, "Of whom speaketh the prophet this? of himself, or of some other man?" (Acts 8:34). The other Man is well known indeed to those of us who have been brought to trust the Man Christ Jesus, who gave Himself a ransom for all. In Him we have beheld the Lamb of God who taketh away the sin of the world (John 1:29).

The Sheep Gate clearly speaks to us, then, of the Cross. It was at the Sheep Gate the Lord met the palsied man and healed him, as recorded in John 5, as it is at the Cross the helpless sinner finds life and peace. Here the remnant of old began to build the wall, priestly hands piling stone upon stone, and setting up the beams and bars. And here every one must begin who has really to do with God, other than in judgment. The wall, we have already seen, speaks of holiness, which must shut out evil; but what evil is, we can never rightly know until we have understood in some measure the meaning of the Cross. It was there that all the iniquity of man's heart was fully revealed; there too that the absolute holiness of God's character was declared in an even more marked way than it will be made known in the lake of fire. In the Cross it was that mercy and truth met together, and that righteousness and peace kissed each other (Ps. 85:10).

"'Tis in the cross of Christ we see How God can save, yet righteous be."

The most important truth of Scripture is, that on the cross the judgment of a holy God against sin fell upon His spotless Son, when He "suffered, the Just for the unjust, that He might bring us to God" (1 Pet. 3:18). There is nothing like the apprehension of this to give peace to a troubled soul. I have been awakened to see myself a lost, guilty sinner. Perhaps for years I have been going about to establish my own righteousness, and trusting that ail would surely be well with me because of fancied merit in myself. I have deluded myself with the notion that God, who is love, must therefore allow sin to pass unpunished, or that my sin was, at any rate, of weight so light it would never sink me down to the pit of woe. But now all is changed. I have learned that I am a lost man! My sins, which once seemed like trifles, insignificant as molehills, now rise before my terrified vision as dark, shapeless mountains, which I fear will bury me beneath their awful weight in the nethermost depths of the abyss of divine wrath. I look on my right hand, but I find no helper. Refuge fails me. In my despair I cry out, "No man cares for my soul l" (Ps. 142:4); and in the hour of my deepest distress there comes to me One with feet beautiful upon the mountains, a messenger, one among a thousand, who tells me the good news that God, the God whom I have so grievously sinned against and so flagrantly dishonored, has found a ransom, and can thus deliver me from going down into the pit (Job 33:24). My sins and guilt have all been laid on Jesus. My judgment has fallen upon His holy head, and thus I can go righteously free.

Well does such a message deserve the name of "gospel!" Good news indeed! More welcome than cold water to a thirsty soul!

As of old, when Noah took of every clean beast and of every clean fowl, and offered burnt-offerings upon the altar (Gen. 8:20), so now Jehovah has looked upon the work of His beloved Son and "smelled a sweet savor," which is truly a "savor of rest" (margin); for sin is thus canceled, and God can be just and the Justifier of him that believeth in Jesus. Christ thus becomes the Door of the sheep, as He said: "I am the door; by Me if any man enter in, he shall be saved, and shall go in and out, and find pasture" (John 10:9).

Of all this, and more also, may the Sheep Gate remind us. A gate of judgment it is too; for of judgment, in Scripture, the gate often speaks, as in Oriental cities it was there that justice was administered. But here it is judgment falling, not upon the guilty, but upon the guiltless One who voluntarily stood in the place of the sinner. "He was delivered for our offences, and raised again for our justification; therefore being justified by faith, we have peace with God through our Lord Jesus Christ" (Rom. 4:25; 5:1).

All thus justified are now the sheep of the Good Shepherd who died, the Great Shepherd who lives in glory, the Chief Shepherd who is coming again. As His sheep, they have title to enter in through the gate into the city. It is saved souls, *and they alone,* who here on earth are gathered by the Spirit to the name of the Lord Jesus in separation from the world and its evil, and it is such alone who will be within that wall of jasper gathered around the Lamb in the glory.

Let me press it upon the reader—has all this been made good to your soul? Is your confidence for eternity based upon the work of Christ? Are you trusting alone in Jesus, who in those solemn hours of deeper than Egyptian darkness, "fought the fight alone," vanquished Satan's power in resurrection, and is now exalted at God's right hand to be a Prince and a Saviour?

Oh, be persuaded! If you are resting on anything short of this, your soul is in peril most grave and fearful; for it is only "the blood of Jesus Christ, God's Son, that cleanses from all sin" (1 John 1:7). If, however, this is the ground of your confidence, if you are saved and know it, if the lesson of the Sheep Gate has been truly learned in the presence of God, I ask you to pass on with me now to

The Fish Gate

But on the way there is a small portion of the wall being built by the men of Jericho. Jericho was the city of the curse, but "Christ hath redeemed us from the curse of the law, being made a curse for us; as it is written, Cursed is every one that hangeth on a tree." So these happy Jericho men are now in the place of blessing, and serving in newness of spirit. Next to them builds, apparently alone, Zaccur, the son of Imri, but God's eye is upon him, and he shall find his name on the honor roll in the day of Christ. Then we read: "But the Fish Gate did the sons of Hassenaah build, who also laid the beams thereof, and set up the doors thereof, the locks thereof and the bars thereof" (ver. 3).

The name of this port at once brings to mind the word of the Lord addressed to Simon and Andrew when He found them "casting a net into the sea." "He saith unto them, Follow Me, and I will make you fishers of men." Precious it is to learn that, without a word as to delay, they *"straightway* left their nets and followed Him" (Matt. 4:17-20).

It is a weighty truth, often I fear forgotten in this pushing, restless age, that the great business of those already saved should be to bring others to Christ. Alas, alas, the indifference as to this among many of the people of God is most appalling! The Fish Gate is closed, or fallen in ruins, and there are no devoted "sons of Hassenaah" who are enough in earnest about the condition of the lost to build it up again. Is it not a shame, a crying shame, that it should ever be true of saints going to heaven, that they are unconcerned about sinners going to hell? And God has said, "He that withholdeth corn, the people shall curse him."

Oh, the heartlessness of it! Souls perishing under one's very eyes, and no voice raised to proclaim God's message of love to the lost! Brothers, sisters, be honest with God! Face the question in His presence, *What are you doing for souls?* Will friends, neighbors, relatives, rise up in that day and say: "I lived beside him for years; he knew I was going to hell; he never warned me, nor told me of a way of escape." I beseech you, don't turn it aside with pious expressions about, "So much fleshly energy," and "the need of building up the saints." Words like these from men who lift not a finger to keep others from going down to eternal ruin, are disgusting indeed; yea, they are worse; they are actually wicked and abhorrent in the ears of Him who saith, "He that is wise winneth souls" (R. V.).

Build up the Fish Gate, brethren; go out after the lost, and bring them inside the wall, where, having been saved, they will be cared for and helped in the things of God.

I know all have not the same gift; all cannot preach to thousands. But surely it is not gift that is lacking so much as grace. It takes no special gift to distribute gospel tracts, or speak a loving word in season to needy souls. If you have "gift" enough to spend hours talking about the weather, or the various questions of domestic, business, or political life, you have all the gift that is needed to drop a

24

tender, warning message in the ear of a careless one, or to point an anxious person to Christ.

Let none shirk this work, for the day of manifestation draws on apace. Then His eyes that are as a flame of fire will pierce into every hidden motive, every unworthy, selfish thought, and bring all to light. In verse 4 we read of three who repaired the stretch of wall adjoining the Fish Gate, and then we read of the Tekoites; and the Holy Ghost has noted that "their nobles put not their necks to the work of their Lord" (ver. 5). They will have to face this record at the judgment-seat of Christ; and I fear there are some God-made, and many self-made, "nobles" among the people of the Lord to-day who manifest as gross indifference to the work of God.

That, on the other hand, mere fleshly zeal will not be owned of God, I quite admit; and this brings before us the need of enforcing the lessons suggested by the next five gates.

The Old Gate

"Moreover the old gate repaired Jehoiada the son of Paseah, and Meshullam the son of Besodeiah; they laid the beams thereof, and set up the doors thereof, and the locks thereof, and the bars thereof."

One would not try to be too insistent on the special meaning of this gate. I had thought of it as the old used in the new, the place of nature in the economy of grace; for our bodies, with all their marvelous members, belong to the old creation still; but He who will glorify them by and by finds use for them in His own service even now in the day of their humiliation.

But the suggestion of another that the old gate would be the port of entry for the old path seems a clearer and higher thought. It is in Jeremiah 6:16 that we read: "Thus saith the Lord, Stand ye in the ways, and see, and ask for the old paths, where is the good way, and walk therein, and ye shall find rest to your souls." And so the Old Gate might speak of subjection to the revealed will of God—abiding in that which was from the beginning. This still impresses upon us the great truth that we are called to recognize in all things the Lordship of Christ, and to hold every power we possess at His command, serving with grace in the heart.

"Naught that I have mine own I call,

I hold it for the Giver;

My heart, my strength, my life, my all,

Are His and His forever."

Evil is not in natural things themselves, but is in the abuse of them. Every talent we have is to be used for His glory. Woe to the man who hides one of them away, under pretence that nature, in this sense, is opposed to grace!

This is what the Holy Spirit presses upon us when He says: "I beseech you therefore, brethren, by the mercies of God, that you present your bodies a living sacrifice, holy, acceptable unto God, which is your reasonable service" (Rom. 12:1). The child of God should remember that he has been bought with a price. His body is purchased with the blood of Christ. He is not merely called to "consecrate" himself, as people put it to-day, but to gladly own that he is already consecrated by the death of the Lord Jesus. The blood and the oil have been placed on the ear, the hand and the foot—he belongs to Christ. The ear, to listen for

His commandment; the hand, to do His bidding; the foot, to run in His ways (see Lev. 14:14-18, 25, 28, 29).

Can anyone truly enter into this, and yet be careless in regard to service? Impossible. You are not only saved from hell, but purchased to be the bondman of Jesus Christ.

There is a depth of meaning in that word "present," as noted above. Your body is His already. He might simply demand His own; but in grace He says, "I beseech you... present your body." Have you done so? Have you, in other words, owned His claims upon you? If not, will you longer delay? O beloved, yield yourself unto Him, that thus you may bring forth fruit unto God. "Herein is My Father glorified, that ye bear much fruit" (John 15:8).

I do not press it that the Old Gate was meant to teach this special truth, and I trust none will find fault over an application.

Whatever the meaning one more spiritually-minded may discern, the fact remains that "Ye are not your own; ye are bought with a price." It is this I seek to emphasize, for it is with many, well-nigh forgotten. Vast numbers of Christians live as though their only thought was to enjoy the present scene, "on the east of Jordan;" pampering every whim of their blood-purchased bodies, and looking forward to going to heaven at last without having ever known the toil and conflict—yet the deep, hidden joy—of the servant's path.

Especially is this often so of those in comfortable and easy circumstances. The willing workers of verse 8 might well rebuke such. "Next unto him repaired Uzziel the son of Harhaiah of the goldsmiths. Next unto him also repaired Hananiah the son of one of the apothecaries." I question if goldsmiths' and apothecaries' sons had known much of downright hard labor, but here we see them hard at work helping to fortify Jerusalem. God has not forgotten that their soft white hands became hardened and sun-burned as they used trowel and mortar on the walls of the holy city.

Nor would I pass over the Gibeonites, Melatiah and the men of Gibeon (ver. 7), whether by these are to understand descendants of the once wily deceivers who entrapped Joshua into disobedience, or Israelites indeed, dwelling in the ancient city. In either case, we may be reminded of what we once were, and what grace has made us.

After the goldsmiths and the apothecaries, repaired Rephaiah, the son of Hur, ruler of half of Jerusalem. He did not hire a servant to do the work for him, but though a man of wealth and power, he labored with his hands, and the Lord took note of his devotedness.

In verse 10 we read of a man whose sphere of labor was very circumscribed but very necessary. Jedaiah repaired "over against his house." This is noteworthy. Many of God's people can do little in a public way in His service, but they can each be concerned about maintaining the wall over against their own houses. And this is tremendously important. It is useless to talk of separation in the assembly, if there be not separation maintained at home. If the children are allowed to go into the world, or to bring the world into the home, depend upon it, the public testimony will avail for little. Godly words in the meeting and worldly ways in the house, will soon disgust neighbors and friends, and prove the undoing of the household.

Another edifying spectacle is afforded us in verse 12: "Next unto him repaired Shallum the son of Halohesh, the ruler of the half part of Jerusalem, *he and his daughters.*" It must have been a grand sight to behold this ruler and his daughters so zealously affected in a good thing. Our sisters have here a bright example of devotedness to the Lord. Would that it might be followed by thousands more!

Oft-times, one fears, where the truth is known that women are called upon to be in subjection, and not to lead in public work (after the fashion of the day), there is a settling down on the part of many sisters to a life of inaction and spiritual desuetude. But all work is not of a public character, as we have already had occasion to observe. There are many ways and abundant opportunities afforded godly women to labor, both in the gospel and in building up the wall of protection and exclusion of evil, without appearing on the platform and usurping authority over the man. Let there be but a willing mind, and it will not be necessary to bewail the lack of opportunities for women's service in a scriptural way.

But if any are to be used of God, there must be not only this recognizing of His claims upon us, but also that lowliness of spirit that ever commends a servant. So we pass on to

The Valley Gate.

"The valley gate repaired Hanun, and the inhabitants of Zanoah" (ver. 13).

This surely suggests humility—a willingness to take a lowly place that thus the Lord may be exalted. One fears it is a gate little used by many of us nowadays.

Pride is ever characteristic of fallen creatures, who have nothing to be proud of; for "what hast thou that thou hast not received?" Even in connection with service for the

Lord, how this unholy thing creeps in, leading one servant to be jealous of another, instead of catching the Master's voice as He says, "What is that to thee? Follow *thou* Me!"

What Cowper says of sin in general may be predicated of pride in particular:

"It twines itself about my thoughts, And slides into my prayer."

It is indeed the root-sin of all. By it Satan himself fell, and one "being lifted up with pride, falls into the condemnation of the devil."

God has said, "To this man will I look; to him that is humble, and of a contrite spirit, and that trembleth at My word." It is perhaps merely a truism to write that only as one walks humbly before Him, is he in a condition of soul to be safely used in service. I do not mean that God cannot overrule all things, and in a sense use even the basest of men. The devil himself has to serve. God used Balaam, and others equally ungodly. But in such cases it is to the condemnation of the very one used.

To go on preaching and handling the truth of God while the heart is lifted up and the eyes lofty is one of the most dangerous courses one can take, and certain to end in ruin and disaster.

We have much cause, as we contemplate our coldness and indifference, and the appalling power of the world over us, to be on our faces before God, instead of walking in pride, only to learn eventually that He "is able to abase" us, as in the case of Babylon's haughty king. If we humble not ourselves, He must humble us in His own way, for it is part of His purpose to "hide pride from man."

Keeping this, then, before our minds, we pass on to the solemn and much-needed lesson of

The Dung Gate.

"But the dung gate repaired Malchiah the son of Rechab, the ruler of part of Beth-haccerem" (ver. 14). Humbling work this, for a ruler, but necessary labor surely.

The Dung Gate was the port whence they carried forth the filth, that the city might not be defiled. And so we read, "Having therefore these promises, dearly beloved, let us cleanse ourselves from all filthiness of the flesh and spirit, perfecting holiness in the fear of God" (2 Cor. 7:1).

Real blessing there cannot be if this is forgotten; but if we have truly learned the lesson of the Valley Gate, that of the Dung Gate will be no difficulty. As saints and servants we are called, not to uncleanness, but to holiness. We are to cleanse ourselves; that is, to judge, in the presence of God, and turn away from, all filthiness—let its form be the grosser one of the flesh, or the less objectionable (in the eyes of men) of the spirit.

In the first three chapters of Romans we have sharply delineated the naked hideousness of the filthiness of the flesh. In the first three chapters of 1st Corinthians and in the 2nd of Colossians, we have unveiled the filthiness of the spirit: a mind exalting itself against God and His Christ—a wisdom that is earthly, sensual, devilish. So we read elsewhere of the "desires of the flesh and of the mind," in which we *once* walked. (See Eph. 2.)

From all these things we are now called to cleanse ourselves. Body and mind alike are to be preserved free from impurity, for the glory of God.

"Flee also youthful lusts" is a much-needed word. In the world about us, men live to pander to the lust of the flesh, and the lust of the eyes, and the pride of life. It should be otherwise with the Christian, and must be otherwise if he is to be a vessel unto honor, sanctified and meet for the Master's use, and prepared unto every good work. Down with the bars of the Dung Gate, brethren; out with the filth! "Be ye clean that bear the vessels of the Lord."

Thus we pass on our journey round the walls, and come next to

The Gate Of The Fountain.

"The gate of the fountain repaired Shallun the son of Colhozeh, the ruler of part of Mizpah" (ver. 15).

To the woman at the well, the Lord Jesus spoke of a fountain (not merely a well) of living water. Again in John 7 He cried, "He that believeth on Me... out of his inward parts shall flow rivers of living water." The fountain of living water is a type, or symbol of the Holy Spirit who indwells all believers.

It has been asserted by many that until the Christian surrenders himself fully to God, he does not receive the gift of the Holy Ghost. This is a mistake. "If any man have not the Spirit of Christ, he is none of His" (Rom. 8:9); "After that ye believed, ye were sealed with that Holy Spirit of promise" (Eph. 1:13)—sealed, too, "until the day of redemption" (Eph. 4:30); "Because ye are sons, God hath sent forth the Spirit of His Son into your hearts" (Gal. 4:6).

But that there is often in the experience of many what looks, indeed, like a "second blessing," no observant believer can deny. What is really meant by it? Simply this: that though the Holy Spirit indwells all children of God in this dispensation, yet, in many, worldliness and self-pleasing are so characteristic, that He who should control us for Christ, and fill us with freshness and power as He ministers Christ to our souls, is become like a fountain choked with stones and rubbish, and thus the life is barren and the testimony powerless. Awakened at last to see the folly of such a life of uselessness to God and reproach to Christ, the saint humbles himself in self-judgment, the filth is put away, and now the once-choked fountain is running over, and the Spirit of God in power takes control of the believer to use him for the Lord's glory, and to make him a vessel of refreshment to others. There is a fountain of living water within, and out of his inward parts flow rivers of living water for others (John 7:38).

"Be ye filled with the Spirit" is a word the importance of which cannot be over-estimated. May every child of grace go on to know more of it in power as he walks in obedience to the word of God! For there are two things that in Scripture are practically inseparable—I refer to the Spirit and the Word. A Spirit-filled Christian will be a Scripture-filled Christian.

In verses 16 to 25 we read of many persons who repaired that portion of the wall extending from the fountain gate to the water gate. There are fine shades and significant expressions used in several instances that we do well to notice. Of one and another we only read that they repaired such and such a portion. In verse 20, of Baruch we are told that he "*earnestly* repaired the other piece, from the turning of the wall," etc. It is not for nothing God inserted that adverb. Three are mentioned in verse 23 who repaired over against their houses, and we can be sure every detail was precious to God. But passing on to verse 26 we reach

The Water Gate.

33

"Moreover the Nethinim dwelt in Ophel, unto the place over against the water gate toward the east, and the tower that lieth out."

The Nethinim were servants, and it is meet that they should have the care of this gate, for water is very generally a type of the word of God. "Wherewithal shall a young man cleanse his way?

By taking heed thereto according to Thy word" (Ps. 119:9).

We do not read of any repairs being made here, only that the Nethinim dwelt over against the water gate. Possibly this port needed none. At any rate, we know that of which it speaks needs not to be repaired, for the word of God liveth and abideth forever. All vain man's assaults upon it have left it uninjured and unchanged. We are called upon to defend it, contending earnestly for the faith once for all delivered to the people of God, but it would be impiety to attempt to patch or improve it.

The water of the Word it is that Christ uses to wash His disciples' feet and to keep them free from defilement (Jno. 13:1-16; 15:3). It is written: "Christ also loved the Church and gave Himself for it, that He might sanctify and cleanse it by the washing of water by the Word," etc. (Eph. 5:25, 26.)

It is remarkable that what in Ephesians is connected with the Spirit, is in Colossians linked with the Word. Compare Eph. 5:18-20 with Col. 3:16. Both alike are a source of joy and blessing. And we need not wonder at this similarity in effect, for of the Word it is said, "Holy men of God spake as they were moved by the Holy Ghost."

In chapter 8 of this book (Nehemiah) we see all the people gathered together "as one man into the street that was before the water gate," there to listen to the reading of the word of God. The result is joy and blessing.

O fellow-believer, I beseech you, "meditate on these things, give thyself wholly to them," and thus shall your profiting appear to all, as you "let the word of Christ dwell in you richly," for, "All Scripture is given by inspiration of God, and is profitable for doctrine, for reproof, for correction, for instruction in righteousness, that the man of God may be perfect, thoroughly furnished unto all good works" (2 Tim. 3:16,17). This, then, is the servant's furnishing. He is to study to show himself "approved unto God, a workman that needeth not to be ashamed, rightly dividing the word of truth."

And this means far more than reading books, however helpful, written on the Bible. It necessitates diligent, painstaking study of the sacred Word itself. Other books may help, often, to lead out the mind on certain broad lines, but *the* Book must supersede them all if there is to be real growth in the knowledge of God.

By this alone will you overcome the wicked one, if "the word of God abideth in you" (1 John 2:14).

Another company of Tekoites repaired between the water gate and that which next claims our attention, namely:

The Horse Gate.

"From above the horse gate repaired the priests, every one over against his house" (ver. 28).

The horse is used with striking frequency in Scripture as a figure of the warrior.

It is so described in Job 39:19-25, where, "He saith among the trumpets, Ha, ha! and he smell-eth the battle afar off."

In Zechariah 1:8, and in Rev. 6, we read of four symbolic horses, which speak of warrior powers; and when the eternal Word of God, clad in blood-dipped vesture, descends from heaven to the battle preceding the awful supper of the great God, at the beginning of the Millennium, He is seen in vision riding on a white horse, and the saints are seen similarly mounted.

The ass is the symbol of peace; the horse, of war. When the Prince of Peace rode into Jerusalem of old, it was on the ass. When He comes to judgment, it is on the horse.

The Horse Gate may speak, then, of soldier-service in a world opposed to God and His truth. It bids us "earnestly contend for the faith once for all delivered to the saints" (Jude 3, R. V.).

The truth has been given to us at great cost, not only to the One who is Himself "the Truth," but for its preservation, and recovery when lost at times, myriads of warrior-saints have suffered and died.

Alas that we, children of such glorious sires, should so lightly value what to them was dearer than life! We live in a day not of open persecution, but of laxity and latitudinarianism. We are affected much by the spirit of the times; hence there are few among us who, like that mighty man of old, grasp the sword of the Spirit to defend the truth of God, and fight till the hand cleaves to the very weapon it holds. (See 2 Sam. 23:9, 10.) But God's Eleazars will have rich reward in the day when many, we fear, will be saved but so as by fire.

Let me quote here the words of another, which might well be written in letters of living fire:

"Renounce all the policy of the age. Trample upon Saul's armor. Grasp the Book of God. Trust the Spirit who wrote its pages. Fight with this weapon only and always. Cease to amuse, and seek to arouse. Shun the clap of a delighted audience, and listen for the sobs of a convicted one. Give up trying to *please* men who have only the thickness of their ribs between their souls and hell; and warn, and plead, and entreat, as those who feel the waters of eternity creeping upon them."[3]

And remember, beloved, as you fight, that the day of testimony for God is fast passing away. It will soon be too late to stand for the truth, and too late to minister Christ to needy souls. "The night cometh when no man can work" (John 9:4).

Of this we are reminded as we pass on to

The East Gate.

"After him repaired also Shemaiah the son of Shechaniah, the keeper of the east gate" (ver. 29).

The gate of the sunrising points on—does it not?—to the morning without clouds, when He shall come down like rain upon the mown grass, and as clear shining after rain.

Having shone forth as the Bright and Morning Star, and as such gathered His redeemed to Himself in the clouds, He will be manifested to Israel and the nations that are spared as the all-glorious Sun of Righteousness, with healing in His wings. This is the special character in which He is presented to Israel and the earth, but the two are only different aspects of His one coming again.

For that glad morning weary saints all along have waited and longed, straining their eyes to catch the first glimpse of the Bright and Morning Star. Wicked servants have said, "My Lord delayeth His coming;" but He "is not slack, as some men count slackness, but is long-suffering to usward, not willing that any should perish" (2 Pet. 3:9). "The night is far spent, the day is at hand." It is high time to be aroused from our lethargy, for already the long-expected midnight cry is ringing through the world, "Behold, the Bridegroom cometh; go ye out to meet Him!" The shout of the Lord, the voice of the arch- angel, and the trump of God, will soon resound through the vaulted heavens, announcing the return of the long-absent One, and ushering in the morning. But for many it will be the beginning of the darkest night earth has ever known.

Oh, let us be up and doing while it is called to-day, that we may not be ashamed before Him at His coming. "Even so, come, Lord Jesus."

Only a small part of the wall remains to be noticed, but among the workers upon it there is one we must not cursorily pass by. Meshullam the son of Berechiah repaired, we learn, "over against his chamber" (ver. 30). Here was a man who probably had no house, no real home. He was but a lodger; but even so, he was faithful to Him who appointed him to glorify God in that narrow place. He went to work with energy and repaired over against his one little room. And thus he becomes a bright example for every one in like circumstances, bidding such remember that "he that is faithful in that which is least, is faithful also in much."

The Gate Miphkad

"After him repaired Mal-chiah the goldsmith's son unto the place of the Nethinim, and of the merchants, over against

38

the gate Miphkad, and to the going up of the corner" (ver. 31).

The word Miphkad, according to the dictionaries, means review, or appointment (for judgment). It was doubtless the gate where controversies were tried, after the Eastern fashion. How solemn is this! For it is when the Lord comes that "we must all appear before the judgment-seat of Christ." That will be the Gate Miphkad for the believer. There will be the last great review. Every detail of the saint's life will come up for inspection. It may be then that,

"Deeds of merit, as we thought them,

He will show us were but sin;

Little acts we had forgotten,

He will tell us were for Him."

Oh, the unspeakable solemnity of it! All our ease-loving and self-seeking brought to light then! All our pride and vanity manifested! Everything put on its own proper level. All our works inspected by Him who seeth not as man seeth. How many of us will wish we had been more true and real in our work down here. Things we valued highly on earth, how lightly will they weigh up there!—as the very small dust of the balance; yea, lighter even than that— altogether, lighter than vanity!

And those things we have neglected and foolishly ignored in the days of our pilgrimage, how much more precious than gold will they appear in the light of that judgment-seat!

O beloved, shall we not seek to be *now* what we shall then wish we had been? Let us do now what we shall then wish we had done; turn now from what we shall then wish we had judged. The Lord grant that His people be awakened to the reality of these things, and the importance of living for eternity!

And thus we have traveled round the wall from one part to another, and have, I trust, been blessed in doing so. We might close our meditations here, only that God does not end in this way, for in the last verse we come back again, having made the circuit, to that with which we began—

The Sheep Gate.

"And between the going up of the corner unto the Sheep Gate repaired the goldsmiths and the merchants."

It is as though God would not have us turn away without reminding us that the Cross with which we began will be before our souls for eternity. After all has been gone into at the judgment-seat, we shall turn from it to the Judge Himself, who is our Redeemer and Bridegroom. We shall see Him as a Lamb that had been slain. At His once-pierced feet we shall fall in adoration, and forever sing praises "unto Him that loveth us, and hath washed us from our sins in His own blood."

We shall never get beyond the Cross. It will be the theme of our praises throughout all the ages to come. Oh, to ever live in the light of it now! It speaks of sins forever put away, and also of a world under judgment for the rejection of God's Son. Our place, then, is outside of it all. "Let us go forth therefore unto Him outside the camp, bearing His reproach. For here have we no continuing city, but we seek one to come" (Heb. 13:13, 14).

40

Chapter IV Soldier-Servants

The work which was so precious in the eyes of the Lord was but a theme for mockery and scorn in the mind of the mixed people, whose overtures of participation on common ground had been refused. Sanballat's rage is stirred; but for the present it takes outwardly the form of contemptuous sneering: "What do these feeble Jews?" he asks his Samaritan brethren. "Will they fortify themselves? will they sacrifice? will they make an end in a day? will they revive the stones out of the heaps of rubbish which are burned?" And Tobiah the Ammonite joins in the mockery, exclaiming with a lightness he evidently did not feel, "Even that which they build, if a fox go up, he shall even break down their stone wall" (vers. 1-3). Yet he and all his ilk were to prove later that, when guarded by Jehovah's subject servants, it was too strong a wall for such foxes as they to break through.

In the name of the Lord, Nehemiah and his companions built steadily on, and that Name was to prove a strong tower into which the righteous might safely retreat from the malignity of their foes. When the people of God cleave to His Word and exalt His name, they need fear no enemy, human or supernatural. It is *themselves* who are responsible for any breaches made in the wall. It is unbelief and self-will in the people of God that weaken or destroy those battlements against which the enemies outside might batter in vain.

Realizing this in some measure, the people of Judah lift up their hearts to the One whose they were and whom they served. "Hear, 0 our God; for we are despised," they cry; "and turn their reproach upon their own head, and give them for a prey in the land of captivity; and cover not their iniquity, and let not their sin be blotted out from before

Thee; for they have provoked Thee to anger before the builders" (vers. 4, 5). If any feel the difference between this prayer and such as are suited to the Christian in this dispensation of grace, the explanation is involved in the question. That was not the time when grace and sufferance were enjoined. The dispensation of law was still in force, and we must view these utterances from that standpoint. The important thing for us to observe is the way in which the remnant cast themselves wholly upon God. San-ballat, Tobiah, and the rest are *His* enemies, not merely theirs, and they count on Him to deal with them.

And so they prayed and builded, for such is the force of "So built we the wall," in verse 6.

Thus with the help of God the breaches were repaired, for willing hands made light work, and "the people had a mind to work."

But soon the opposition took a different form. When the united nations (notice the lengthened list—Sanballat, Tobiah, the Arabians and the Ammonites, and the Ashdodites) heard that the work was actually nearing completion, and that the wall was being repaired in a substantial manner, their indignation became greater than ever. They had hoped the rubbish would impede the progress of the work to such an extent as to completely dishearten the Jews; but bit by bit this had been cleared away, and the stones uncovered and set in their places. Hence these enemies of what is of God realize something more than mockery is required if they would not soon be effectually shut out of the holy city.

As one reads such a record, it is almost impossible not to observe how accurately the history of old fits a later work of God—even that of the present time. As a result of centuries of darkness and superstition, practically every precious truth of the Scriptures was overwhelmed by the ecclesiastical rubbish gradually accumulated. When at last the reformers were raised up to recall God's people to God's own Word, they found themselves confronted by just such a task as that which Nehemiah had to face; and ever since, when there has been a settling down on the part of God's people, the rubbish has accumulated again at an alarming rate, human tradition soon swamping what was of God; and so the need of persistent, devoted, prayerful toil, to separate the precious from the vile has been ever manifest. Carnal professors will mock, so-called liberals will demonstrate their bitter hatred of everything holy, but they who wait upon the Lord shall renew their strength, and find all needed grace to stand in the evil day, and to distinguish between what is really divine and what is but of man in the great mounds of mingled truth and error, lying all about the ruined wall that once separated Church and world. Every fresh attempt to "try the things that differ" will provoke the ire of the worldly-religious mass; but what is of God is of too much value to be surrendered at the behest of fleshly foes.

The adversaries of Judah determined upon a sudden onslaught on the remnant, and so "conspired all of them together to come and fight against Jerusalem, and to hinder it" (ver. 8). This was but a call to "watch and pray," and so it was recognized by Nehemiah and his fellow-laborers. The language of verse 9 is most instructive: "Nevertheless we made our prayer unto our God, and set a watch against them day and night, because of them." This was holding things in the right proportion. Prayer alone would have been presumption. But they watch against the enemy at the same time that they call upon God.

In verse 10 we have the first note of discouragement from within. Constant toil and watching have worn upon the spirits of the Jews, and so the report comes to Nehemiah: "The strength of the bearers of burdens is decayed, and there is much rubbish; so that we are not able to build the wall." But to these disheartening words Nehemiah vouchsafes no reply, save to labor on. The adversaries continue their plotting without and the people grow faint within, but the Tirshatha continues to look up and count upon the living God.

The third trial is mentioned in verse 12. There were scattered Jews living among the Samaritans. They "came unto us ten times," says Nehemiah, warning of the preparations for an assault, and declaring the utter inability of the remnant to stand against such powerful foes.

It was certainly discouraging to one who relied on a fleshly arm, but the man of faith could count on God through it all. Heretofore the people had labored, prayed, and watched. Now they must be prepared for conflict. So the governor set the people after their families in the vantage-places upon the wall, armed with swords, spears and bows. But he would not have them put their confidence in the weapons, but in the living God: "Be ye not afraid of them; *remember the Lord,* which is great and terrible, and fight for your brethren, your sons, and your daughters, your wives and your houses" (ver. 14). This was to be their battle-cry, "Remember the Lord!"

Many a merely human conflict has been won by the inspiration of a watch-word recalling some past great event. In our own day, again and again, Spanish troops were repulsed as the American soldiery drove all before them with the cry, "Remember the Maine!" So Napoleon often inspirited his troops by causing them to remember some former victory. But what could stir the soul of an Israelite indeed more than such a cry as this, *"Remember the Lord!"* Similarly when pressing upon Timothy the need of devotedness in the Christian warfare, Paul cries, "Remember Jesus Christ!" (2 Tim. 2:8).[4]

This is faith's resource. The God who gave His Son for our redemption, who raised Him from the dead and set Him at His own right hand in highest glory, can be counted on in every time of trial to supply all needed grace for seasonable help.

When Nehemiah's enemies knew that their plans were known, and the citizens of Jerusalem armed and watchful, they gave up all hope of hindering by open warfare; while the remnant rejoiced that "God had brought their counsel to nought;" and so they returned every one with confidence to the work.

But this deliverance did not cause them to be any the less careful. Henceforth Nehemiah divided his own servants into two companies, one of which wrought in the work and the other stood guard heavily armed; while the builders and burden-bearers themselves labored, each with his sword girded by his side, or with a trowel in one hand and a weapon in the other. Both alike speak of the Word. The trowel is the Word used for edification, the sword is the Word used to contend earnestly for the faith once for all delivered to the saints. Significant are the words that close verse 18, after this vivid description of soldier-laborers: "And he that sounded the trumpet was by me." The trumpet stands for the ministry of the Word, and it was meet that the trumpeter should abide with the ruler and get his instructions directly from him. So does the servant of Christ need to abide in Him that he may speak as the oracles of God, and then the trumpet gives no uncertain sound.

Scattered as the workers and soldiers were upon the whole length of the wall, it was important that all should be subject to one voice, the voice of Nehemiah, and this was expressed by the trumpet. Wherever the loud blast was heard, there all were to gather, counting upon God to fight for them (vers. 19, 20).

"So,"[5] continues the inspired record, "we labored in the work: and half of them held the spears from the rising of the morning till the stars appeared."

There was much work to be done and time was pressing, so they dared not take their ease while there was light enough to labor. And at night all lodged within the wall, that they might be a defence to their brethren, though many had homes outside the city.

In all this devoted service, Nehemiah and his guard were ensamples to the rest, for so continuously were they on duty that they did not so much as remove their clothes, save for washing. It was a time to try men's souls, but the testing only proved how zealously affected in a good thing were the governor and his helpers. In this they shine as examples for us, bidding us hold fast what God has committed to us, and hold forth the word of life to others, while refusing all compromise with the unholy spirit of the age in which we live.

Chapter V Internal Strife

Outside foes may rage, but they cannot really injure the people of God if there be love and harmony within. "Only," writes the apostle, "let your conversation (the conduct) be as it becometh the gospel of Christ; that whether I come and see you, or else be absent, I may hear of your affairs, that ye stand fast in one spirit, with one mind striving together for the faith of the gospel; and in nothing terrified by your adversaries: which is to them an evident token of perdition, but to you of salvation, and that of God" (Phil. 1:27, 28). The contrary is involved in the warning given by James: "Where envying and strife is, there is confusion and every evil work" (James 3:16). And this Paul also set before the Galatians, when he wrote: "If ye bite and devour one another, take heed that ye be not consumed one of another" (Gal. 5:15). The sheep of the Lord's flock need to keep close to the Shepherd and to one another if they would be guarded from the prowling wolves who ever seek their destruction. But how sad, and what shame it is when they fall to devouring one another, thus giving place to the devil. Of this we are warned in the happenings narrated for our instruction in this chapter.

The opening verses are like Acts 6:1: "There was a great cry of the people and of their wives against their brethren the Jews. For there were that said, We, our sons and daughters, are many, and we must procure corn for them that we may eat, and live. Some also there were that said, We have mortgaged our lands, vineyards and houses, that we might buy corn in the dearth. There were also that said, We have borrowed money for the king's tribute, and that upon our lands and vineyards. Yet now our flesh is as the flesh of our brethren, our children as their children; and, lo, we bring into bondage our sons and our daughters to be servants, and some of our daughters are brought into bondage already; neither is it in our power to redeem them; for other men have our lands and vineyards" (vers. 1-5).

What a pitiable state of affairs is portrayed here by the simple narrative of the complaints of the people against their own brethren! The worst of it all was, that the accusations were true; and the demands of the usurers were, so far as business principles are concerned, such as all nations recognize as legitimate. But God's people were not to be guided by such principles. From the beginning He had told them not to exact usury of their brethren, but rather to make provision for the poor, as giving unto Him. They had all been in poverty once, and He had enriched them according to the grace of His heart, not according to their deserts. Alas, how soon had they forgotten this when it came to dealing with one another.

And what sorrows have come upon the children of God in all dispensations because of this very thing! The full manifestation of grace in the present age has not hindered the same mercenary spirit often appearing among those who owe all to the mercy of God. We have already referred to Acts 6; and the conditions prevailing in the assembly at Corinth, long after, were the fruit of a similar state. Brother dragged brother to law, and that before the unjust—men who, whatever their reputation in the world, were not suited to deal with things in the Church. How incongruous are such conditions with the grace of Christianity!

Nor is it only in connection with temporal things that such a spirit has been manifested, but, alas, in fancied zeal for the holy things of God how often has the same evil principle of exaction prevailed. Questions have arisen in

48

Christian assemblies, often of the most perplexing character, concerning which an almost instantaneous judgment has been demanded; and if tried souls and weak gatherings have not been able to bow to the *ipse dixit* of certain carnal leaders, excision or excommunication have been resorted to, in defiance of the word of God and the Spirit of Christ. What is all this but the same thing prevailing in spiritual matters which wrought so much havoc in these temporal affairs?

Oh for more men who, instead of tacitly acquiescing in these unholy conditions, are stirred to a righteous anger by such un-Christlike ways! Nehemiah's upright and unselfish soul was moved to indignation, and with the assurance that came from knowing he sided with God, he rebuked the nobles and the rulers for thus exacting usury of their brethren. The matter was brought up for open consideration in a "great assembly," and the guilt of the leaders charged home upon their consciences before all the people. "We," he says, "after our ability, have redeemed our brethren the Jews, which were sold unto the heathen; and will ye even sell your *brethren?* or shall they be sold unto us?" They were speechless; what answer could they make?

Apply it to conditions such as I have referred to above. Think of the toil and labor that have been expended by devoted servants of Christ to bring lost sinners to His feet. Think of the ministry exercised afterwards to lead on these young converts and establish them in the truth. Think of the pastoral care exercised by earnest, faithful men who knew them as individual members of the flock of Christ—not as a mass without heart or conscience—and then think of the spirit of exaction that can press some test-question on such saints, and ruthlessly cut off and cast

49

out souls for whose blessing others have labored so persistently—and this by men who profess to act for God and to seek His glory!

Oh, brethren, let us listen to the words of Nehemiah and bow our head in the dust if we have been parties to such unholy ways. "It is *not* good that ye do: ought ye not to walk in the fear of our God because of the heathen our enemies? I likewise, and my brethren, and my servants, might exact of them money and corn: *I pray you, let us leave off this usury.* Restore, I pray you, to them, even this day, their lands, their vineyards, their oliveyards, and their houses, also the hundredth part of the money, and of the corn, the wine, and the oil that ye exact of them" (vers. 9-11).

These are suited words for the present solemn time when God has been exercising many as to the very things of which we have been speaking. It is not a time to demand the uttermost farthing of one another, but rather to heed the word, "I pray you, let us leave off this usury." If we have been guilty of robbing any of our brethren of their blood-bought privileges, let us hasten to restore what we can ere the Lord arise as their champion and we be put to shame. For He has said, "Hear the word of the Lord, ye that tremble at His word; Your brethren that hated you, that cast you out for My name's sake, said, Let the Lord be glorified; but He shall appear to *your joy,* and *they* shall be ashamed" (Isa. 66:5). Cutting and comforting words are these mingled by the Lord Himself. Oh, for a heart to take heed to them ere it be forever too late!

On the part of the rulers in Judah there was an instant response when the words of Nehemiah had moved them to repentance. "Then said they, We will restore them, and will require nothing of them; so will we do as thou sayest" (ver.

12). And this was sealed with an oath, and further confirmed by a graphic action on the part of the Tirshatha. He shook his lap and said, "So God shake out every man from his house, and from his labor, that performeth not this promise, even thus be he shaken out, and emptied." And this was attested by the solemn "Amen!" of the congregation, who praised the Lord for the mercy shown. It was the same spirit that led the apostle Paul, long afterwards to write: "I would they were even cut off that trouble you!"

In the closing verses, Nehemiah contrasts his own behaviour with that which he had so severely censured. One is again reminded of Paul. It was an occasion where he was compelled to "speak as a fool" that he might close the mouths of any gainsayers. He relates how that from the day of his appointment as governor he had never availed himself of the perquisites of his office, that he might not be burdensome to the people whose blessing he sought.

Former governors had felt free to do this, but the fear of God restrained him from doing the same. Instead, he had kept open house for a hundred and fifty of the Jews and rulers, besides strangers from the surrounding villages. He was one who had learned that "it is more blessed to give than to receive," and he acted accordingly. The people might forget all this—alas, too often do; but he cries, "Think upon me, my God, for good, according to all that I have done for this people" (ver. 19). This may seem to savor of self-complacency, but who of us would dare judge so devoted a servant? And again we need to remind ourselves that the dispensation of grace had not yet dawned. Law was still in the ascendant, and the spirit shown by Nehemiah is so beyond his age that we can only give thanks for what God had wrought in the soul of His dear servant, while we pray for wisdom and grace to serve His people in our own generation unselfishly, and in the Spirit of Christ, leaving all question of appreciation or reward to be settled at His judgment-seat.

Chapter VI Plots And Snares

Again our attention is directed to the opposition of Sanballat, Tobiah, and Geshem (or Gashmu) with the rest of Judah's enemies. Every move within the city was reported to them without, and no doubt they had felt a sense of deep satisfaction when the news of internal strife had reached them. This may account for our having heard nothing of them in the last chapter. If God's people get quarrelling among themselves, the enemy from without can afford to rest in his tents, but as soon as things get right within he actively bestirs himself.

Word having reached the adversaries that the wall was builded and no breach left in it (although the doors had not yet been set up on the gates), Sanballat and Geshem sent an apparently friendly message to Nehemiah, saying, "Come, let us meet together in some one of the villages in the plain of Ono" (ver. 2). They would lure him unto neutral ground, outside the wall, as though to confer on matters of importance; but he recognized the evil purpose of their hearts; he inwardly knew their thought was to do him mischief.

His reply is worthy of the man, and should have a voice for any in our day who are tempted to take neutral ground where the truth of Christ is in question. "I am doing a great work, so that I cannot come down: why should the work cease, whilst I leave it, and come down to you?" He had been entrusted by God with a commission "to restore and build Jerusalem," and he would brook nothing that would for a moment turn him aside from this. A separated man, he would have no part in the surrounding confusion where the word of God was rejected and His people despised. Notice here: it was no question of ministering to, or caring for the children of God scattered abroad that was before him. We may be sure Nehemiah would have been as ready to help the dispersed of Israel as those in Jerusalem. But these Samaritans were the enemies of God's truth, while pretending to serve Him. "They feared the Lord, and served their own gods" (2 Kings 17:33). They represent, as we have seen, unreal professors, yet presuming to have full title to the name and place of worshipers. With such the faithful servant can have no fellowship. He must maintain and guard what has been committed to him, and if he attempts to mix with these "deceitful workers" he will only lose what he himself has.

Four times Sanballat and Geshem sent to Nehemiah "after this sort," and four times he returned the same answer.

Then they changed their tactics. They had tried conciliatory methods and failed to corrupt him. Now they would use a scandalous report with intent to intimidate him. There is nothing new under the sun. Satan's wiles are such that the man of God must not be ignorant of his devices. The fifth time Sanballat sends his servant with "an open letter in his hand." Oh, these "open letters!" How often, while fairly worded, have they been penned only to gender strife. This one contained a covert insinuation to the effect that all Nehemiah's work had been unauthorized, and a direct charge that his object was self-aggrandizement and rebellion against the king. Themselves in rebellion against God, they charge God's servant with their own sin. The "open letter" reads somewhat graciously, but the object of its writer was to occupy the Jews with his apparently gracious spirit in order to poison their minds against Nehemiah. "It is reported among the nations, and Gashmu saith it, that thou and the Jews think to rebel: for which cause thou buildest the wall, that thou mayest be their king, according to these words. And thou hast also appointed prophets to preach of thee at Jerusalem, saying, There is a king in Judah; and now shall it be reported to the king according to these words. Come now, therefore, and let us take counsel together" (vers. 6, 7). Such were the contents of the open letter, and we are not told what impression, if any, it made on the Jews. It was so worded as to intimate that Sanballat's only desire was to clear Nehemiah of the charges whispered about, and yet so cunningly phrased that any disaffected ones within might readily charge the governor with fearing an investigation if he did not go down to confer with Sanballat.

But Nehemiah is not at all concerned about this. He knows he is personally right with God and he fears not suspicion and idle tales. "There are no such things done as thou sayest," he retorts boldly, "but thou feignest them out of thine own heart."

So was it also when evil workers sought to undermine the apostle Paul's influence, and so has it ever been when the truth was hated. To discredit, by fair means or foul, the messenger, is one of Satan's cunning devices in order to discredit the message. To do this, his tools often affect great humility themselves; and pretending to be zealous for the liberty of the people of God, they cry "Pope!" "Diotrephes!" "Heretic!" when any servant of Christ and the Church seeks to stand steadfastly against iniquity, hoping thereby to throw dust in the eyes of simple believers, in order to gain their own unrighteous ends.

Trials like these are not easy to bear. To have one's good evil-spoken of, to be called a "lord over God's heritage" when trying to serve in lowliness, is painful indeed to any sensitive soul. But it is well not to retaliate, nor even to explain, but just to refuse the cowardly charge and leave results with God.

Nehemiah's conscience was free, so he could throw the accusation back upon the man who made it; and knowing it was only done to weaken their hands from the work, he looks heavenward and cries, "Now therefore, O God, strengthen my hands" (ver. 9).

But Satan has not yet exhausted his ammunition. A man is found *within the city* to act for Sanballat and Tobiah, upon the payment of a bribe. Shemaiah, the son of Delaiah, is said to have been "shut up." This probably means that he was ill, or confined to his house, and unable to take his place among the workers on the wall. Such a man, if not in fellowship with God as to His then present ways, would prove a ready tool for the conspirators. Nehemiah called upon him, and Shemaiah warned him with pretended sincerity of danger to his life, counselling that he should flee to the temple, there to seek security by hiding in the sanctuary. To do so would have at once spread fear and distrust among the people, and this was just what Sanballat desired.

But God's devoted servant again rose, strong in faith, superior to the situation. "Should such a man as I flee?" he asks, "and who is there, that, being as I am, would go into the temple to save his life? I will not go in" (ver. 11). To desert the rest and act as though panic-stricken, would ill become one in his position, one who also had confessed his faith in God so boldly. He realized that he was again face to face with evidence of the plots of his enemies, and that God had not sent Shemaiah with such a message, but that he was hired by Tobiah and Sanballat to give this unworthy counsel. With these were others who shared in the conspiracy; one, a prophetess named Noadiah, and

56

several unnamed men, also in the prophetic office. Sad and solemn it is when those who take the place of speaking for God are found in sympathy with the adversaries of His truth, thus hindering the work He has committed to His loyal servants.

Nehemiah, in his customary way, brings the whole matter at once to God, and puts the case in His hands. "My God," he prays, "think Thou upon Tobiah and Sanballat according to these their works, and on the prophetess Noadiah, and the rest of the prophets, that would have put me in fear" (ver. 14). It is no longer a matter between Nehemiah and the conspirators but it is now an affair between God and these unholy plotters. And in His own time He can be depended upon to settle all righteously.

At last, despite every effort to frustrate the work, "the wall was finished" in fifty-two days from the time they began to labor. When this was manifest to the surrounding nations "they were much cast down in their own eyes: for they perceived that this work was wrought of our God" (ver. 16). With what different feelings would the Jewish remnant contemplate the completed wall! Praise and thanksgiving would well up in their breasts, that Jerusalem was once more a protected city.

No doubt the enemy hated such "narrow exclusiveness," and would search eagerly for some small breach whereby to force an entrance, or pass in by night. Judah's exclusiveness was their security. So long as the spirit of the people within answered to the strong wall without, they were safe. Their *position* was now clearly defined. The next question was, Would their *condition* answer to it? Alas, the very next verse manifests a bad state. With some at least, the separation was only outward—not of heart and conscience. How often has this been repeated in the history of God's people!

A position may be taken which outwardly is fully in accord with Scripture; yet the heart may not go with it at all. People *talk* of separation, priding themselves on being in a certain ecclesiastical circle, apart from sects of man's devising, while yet in their homes and in business-life going on with the world as though never separated at all. This is of the very essence of Phariseeism—an outward position rigidly maintained, while inwardly corruption holds sway.

Inside the walls of Jerusalem it was far from being in accord with the position taken. "Moreover in those days the nobles of Judah sent many letters unto Tobiah, and the letters of Tobiah came unto them. For there were many in Judah sworn unto him, because he was the son-in-law of Shechaniah the son of Arah; and his son Johanan had taken the daughter of Meshullam the son of Berechiah. Also they reported his good deeds before me, and uttered my words to him. And Tobiah sent letters to put me in fear" (vers. 17-19). It was a complete overturning of divine order. God had said, "The people shall dwell alone, they shall not be reckoned among the nations." And to so abide was to be strong and be under His protecting hand. But the unequal yoke had been entered into. Mixed marriages, despite the bitter lesson in Ezra's day, were still tolerated and excused; and so conscience was broken down and the nobles of Judah lost all power of discrimination. The wall might separate between them and ungodly Tobiah, but there was no separation in spirit, so they easily found means of communication with the haters of God's truth.

To Nehemiah they prated of the good qualities and benevolence of "brother Tobiah," and to the latter they spoke complainingly of the unnecessary strictness of the governor. They were traitors and hinderers, though occupying positions of prominence among the Jews. "Discerning of spirits" is a gift to be coveted; for dullness of sight is becoming increasingly characteristic of many who once were counted upon as able to discern between good and evil.

When the heart goes with the world and worldly religiousness, all kinds of excuses will be made for those who go on with the mixed condition. Their position and actions—no matter how un-scriptural—will be palliated and explained away; while those who truly go on with God will be subjected to the extremes of criticism, and every word and deed viewed as unfavorably as possible. Hence the need of being deeply exercised as to the inward state, as well as carefully walking in the path outlined in the word of God.

The chapter we have been considering is full of warnings for our own times. Happy those who have ears to hear and hearts to understand.

Mere outward separation, with its accompaniment of breaking bread in scriptural simplicity on the first day of each week, will avail for nothing, if there be not heart-detachment from the world and heart-attachment to the Lord Jesus Christ, leading to holiness of life and self-judgment. Only thus can we keep in any measure the unity of the Spirit in the bond of peace.

Chapter VII Restoring Order

The greater part of this chapter from verse 6 to the end, consists of the register of the genealogy, which has already been considered in our study of the book of Ezra (chap. 2), and which we need not again go over here.

This might seem to leave very little that is new for our present concern; but a careful examination of the five opening verses will reveal much on which we may meditate with profit, as being of marked importance at the present serious moment of our history as saints and servants of God and of our Lord Jesus Christ. The more Nehemiah's record is examined, the more it will be seen that every sentence is pregnant with instruction for these closing days of the dispensation of grace. "Written aforetime," they were, nevertheless, "written for our learning;" and we shall be blessed indeed if we carefully appropriate and earnestly practise the lessons they convey to us.

"Now it came to pass, when the wall was built, and I had set up the doors, and the porters and the singers and the Levites were appointed, that I gave my brother Hanani, and Hananiah the ruler of the palace, charge over Jerusalem; for he was a faithful man, and feared God above many" (vers. 1,2). There are several matters of moment to occupy us in these two verses. The wall, we have seen, speaks of separation—both *from* the world and its evil, and *to* the Lord, the God of Israel. The gates speak, not of unscriptural exclusion that has no heart for those who are of the one family, but of fellowship, admitting to the privileges to be enjoyed within the walls all who have divine title to enter, and barring out all others. And this suggests the importance of Nehemiah's appointment of *porters,* or gate-keepers. He was not indifferent as to who came or went. The business of the porters was to act as watchmen of the gates, permitting only such to come inside as could give evidence of their right so to do.

In applying this to the ordering of the Christian assembly, it is easy to see what an important place the porter occupies. Suppose a company of believers, gathered to the name of the Lord Jesus Christ, in separation from worldly and ecclesiastical evil: how long will its purity and holy character be maintained if people are allowed to come and go as they will without true, godly care as to their new birth, their behavior, the doctrines that they bring, or the associations they go on with? Hence the need of the sometimes unpleasant service of the porter.

I do not mean that certain ones should be ap- pointed as inquisitors of those applying for fellowship ; rather, that all should be duly exercised before God as to who are received to the holy and exalted privileges of Christian fellowship. In the breaking and eating of the loaf, and the drinking of the cup, we not only set forth the Lord's death, and fellowship with Him who thus gave Himself for us, but we thereby manifest our communion or fellowship with those participating with us in this solemn observance. And how can there be fellowship if there be not confidence and unity? Therefore the folly of declaring that, "We examine no one: each must judge himself: none are accountable to others."

Such principles are subversive of Christian communion. We are called upon to discern those who, with us, partake at the table of the Lord. "If any man that is called a brother be a fornicator, or covetous, or an idolator, or a railer, or a drunkard, or an extortioner, with such an one" we are commanded "not to eat" (1 Cor. 5:11). But must we not then examine those called brothers if we are to be obedient to this scripture? And again, "If there come any unto you, and bring not this doctrine" (z. e., the doctrine of Christ), we are told to "receive him not into your house, nor greet him, for he that greeteth him is partaker of his evil deeds" (2 John 10, 11, N.T.). But if the gates be left wide open, and the porter asleep, or off duty, who shall hinder persons—either themselves bringing the evil teaching, or contaminated by known association with it—forcing their way in, to the defilement of the whole company? Hence the need of godly care in receiving to Christian fellowship.

It is sometimes said, "We receive all who are Christ's." But do any really mean this? Who dares pronounce as to those who are Christ's? "The Lord knoweth them that are His" (2 Tim. 2:19). We make a great mistake when we attempt to give oracular decisions as to so momentous a matter. We are only called upon to examine the profession, the life, the doctrine, and, as a matter of course, the associations of the applicant for fellowship. Even then, when all due care has been exercised, a self-deceived one, or a deceiver, may be unwittingly permitted to creep in (Jude 4), to cause serious trouble later; but if there were no porter-service at all, who can conceive the state of things that would soon exist! The world itself is not so foolish as to leave its ports of entry unguarded. It is certainly far easier to allow any who desire to come in unchallenged; but it is neither for their blessing nor the peace of the assembly, not to speak of the glory of the Lord. So it would have been easier in Nehemiah's day to have opened the gates at dawn and left them open till nightfall, with no watchful porter to question persons desiring to enter; but in that case how much of the work we have been considering would have gone for nothing!

The porter at the gate was therefore a person of great importance in Jerusalem, and only discreet and cautious men should have performed this service. And what answers to this in the Christian assembly is the exercise of godly, thoughtful care as to who are permitted to share in the holy things committed to the people of God. Fellowship is worth too much to be frittered away by mere sentimentality. It has been said, "Eternal vigilance is the price of liberty"—and we might say it of Christian fellowship also, which is soon dissipated if the porter's service is overlooked.

The second order established by Nehemiah was that of the *singers.* And they too may give occasion for fruitful meditation. The spirit of praise is the spirit of power. A rejoicing assembly will be one where God is free to work, and will become a channel of blessing to those without. In Israel the singers were a distinct company, separated from the body of the people. But the New Testament contemplates no such incongruity as a choir—surpliced or otherwise—to lead the praises of the assembly. The Lord Jesus Himself is the Leader, and all believers are exhorted to "sing with the spirit and with the understanding also." "Speaking to yourselves in psalms, and hymns, and spiritual songs, singing and making melody in your heart unto the Lord; giving thanks always for all things unto God and the Father in the name of our Lord Jesus Christ" (Eph. 5:19, 20). "Let the word of Christ dwell in you richly in all wisdom; teaching and admonishing one another; in psalms and hymns and spiritual songs, singing with grace in your hearts unto the Lord" (Col. 3:16). In these verses we have clearly set forth the singers, the song, and the accompaniment. All believers are the choristers. The accompaniment is not the grand pipe organ or the delightsome orchestra, but something sweeter far in the ears of God—the melody that rises from a heart filled with His grace.

We may distinguish psalms from hymns. The former would more properly be expressions of praise. To praise is to psalm. (See Ps. 105:2, *margin*). A hymn is rather an ascription of the perfections of Deity; it expresses the highest point of worship, magnifying God, not because of His works in our behalf, but of His matchless perfections. A spiritual song would be different from either of these. It might be a recital of God's ways or of the believer's experience.[6]

When gathered in assembly we come together as singers. There the Lord takes His place in the midst to lead our worship and praise, as it is written, "In the midst of the assembly will I sing praise unto Thee" (Heb. 2:12). Thus, as occupied with Him, His death and the fruit resulting therefrom, praise well becomes each saint. This is not to legislate against every other spiritual exercise, but it is surely what is characteristic.

And now we turn to consider the third class mentioned in the first verse. These are the Levites, or ministering servants of God. Of old one tribe alone were Levites. But in this dispensation, just as all gathered saints have porter-responsibility upon them, and all are to be singers, so all are servants. "To every man his work" is the Lord's word for each. But Levite-service may also speak of public ministry, and this of course is not general, but a special responsibility placed upon those who have been gifted accordingly—yea, who are themselves gifts given to the assembly for the edification of the body of Christ.

Such service must be exercised in direct responsibility to the Lord. The Church does not appoint ministers of the

Word. Christ as Head alone appoints, and by the Spirit qualifies. The Church tests those who come as ministers by the message they bring, comparing it with the word of God. If it be according to what is there revealed it must be accepted. If contrary to the teaching of Scripture, both teacher and doctrine are to be refused.

There is room in every scripturally-gathered company of saints for all divinely-given ministry. The true Levite will find a welcome there. But, after all is said and done, there is no infallible court on earth that can decide whether or no a man is a gift to the assembly. The only rule is that of Prov. 18:16: "A man's gift maketh room for him." Hence, if one fancies he is called to expound the Word, and his ministry is not appreciated, he need not abuse the saints, but should rather consider that among them at least his gift has not made room. He may be a minister to others, but not to them. If assured of his divine call, let him patiently go elsewhere; but let him also carefully consider whether he may not be boasting himself of a false gift, and so cause shame at last, because of the emptiness of his ministry (Prov. 25:14). To serve as a Levite in this special sense, one must be in living touch with God, speaking from a full heart of what has stirred his own soul; otherwise his ministry will be barren and profitless. We shall see the Levites doing their God-appointed service in the interesting scenes of the next chapter.

In the second verse now before us we read of two men placed over Jerusalem. We may be assured it was not nepotism that led Nehemiah to appoint his own brother Hanani as one of these. To have done this because of relationship would have been most offensive. On the other hand relationship must not hinder when spiritual qualification is evident. Of Hananiah, his coadjutor in this service, it is said that "he was a faithful man, and one that feared God above many." Blessed words of commendation are these! Would that they might be rightfully applied to many more of us! What honor could be greater than to be designated faithful by the Lord Himself on His judgment-seat.

These last-mentioned men had authority over the porters, and to them Nehemiah commands: "Let not the gates of Jerusalem be opened until the sun be hot; and while they stand by, let them shut the doors, and bar them; and appoint watches of the inhabitants of Jerusalem, every one in his watch, and every one over against his house" (ver. 3).

Two things concern us here. First:—Entrance into the city was to be in broad daylight. People were not to be permitted to slip in, in the dark. This may have a voice for us. Let all assembly matters especially as concerning reception and excision be open and above-board: nothing underhanded or hidden should be tolerated. Second:— Watchfulness was still required of all. It was not enough to have official porters. All were to be watchmen for the good of all. "What I say unto you, I say unto all: Watch!" As long as we have anything to maintain for God down here we need to be on the watch—never off guard for a moment, lest our wily foe introduce what will cause lasting sorrow and disaster.

The city was large and great, we are told—that is, the space enclosed by the walls; but the people were few, and the houses were not builded. The wall enclosed all that had originally been marked off as the city of God. But the remnant were feeble, and care would be needed to maintain the place taken. In view of giving each one his proper portion Nehemiah now investigates the registry made when the first company came up. It was no new work he was engaged in. He is but carrying on what had been commenced some years before. The original record is therefore examined, and all ratified by the governor. As we have already gone over this register we need only refer the reader to the remarks made in the notes on the 2nd chapter of Ezra.

Its appearance here shows how completely Nehemiah had identified himself with the work which the Spirit of God had wrought through Zerubbabel and Joshua. He was one with them, and together they sought the glory of the God of Israel. Let this have a voice for all who have ears to hear.

Chapter VIII The Great Bible-Reading

In every genuine revival among God's people the revealed Word of the Lord has had a large place. It was so in Josiah's day, and in the awakening under Hezekiah. It has been so throughout the Church period. It was the recovery of the Word that brought about the Reformation of the 16th century, and every true awakening since has been based upon Bible study and Bible practice. Of no spiritual movement in history could this more truthfully be said than of that special work of God which began almost simultaneously in many parts of Great Britain and Ireland in the first half of the 19th century. Here and there little companies of devoted believers were found gathering together to search the Scriptures, seeking a right way for themselves and their children in the midst of the existing ecclesiastical confusion and dead formality. To them was revealed from the Word that Christ Jesus is the one Centre of gathering, that the Church is one body in which the Holy Spirit dwells and which He is to guide. Thus disowning everything for which they could find neither a plain "Thus saith the Lord" nor a simple divine principle exemplified in Scripture, they turned away from all sects and systems to be known only as brethren in Christ, members of His body, seeking to walk in subjection to the Holy Spirit. For such, these remnant books are full of important and much-needed instruction. They have failed—failed grievously and openly—as did the restored Jews of old; but the same resource remains for these as for those—the abiding, unerring word of God. And it is this that is so strikingly set forth in our chapter. There are seven things here brought to our notice, and I desire to write of them in order.

First, it is a united people waiting on God. This is what verse 1 suggests. "All the people gathered themselves together as one man into the open place that was before the Water Gate." We have already observed that the Water Gate intimates something of the cleansing, refreshing, reviving power of the word of God. What more fitting place for a company of people to be in who are seeking divine instruction than "the open place before the Water Gate?" Depend upon it, God will never disappoint His saints when thus before Him. Of old He said to Moses, "Gather the people *together,* and I will give them water" (Num. 21:16). And in a higher sense will that word ever be fulfilled when His people are with one mind and one heart gathered together to learn His will from His all-sufficient Word.

In the second place we hear the cry, "Bring the Book!" Verse 1 goes on to say, "And they spake unto Ezra the scribe to *bring the book* of the law of Moses, which the Lord had commanded to Israel." People may sneer and call this *bibliolatry* if they will. Worship of the book it is *not.* It is rather the acknowledgement that the Author of the Book is the all-wise and all-sufficient One who has so given His Word as to make it a safe guide in every time of confusion. What was it that freed the people of the Lord in the middle ages and overthrew the power of Rome? It was the response to this same cry, "Bring the Book!" And whenever or wherever God's children are thus ready to hear His Word and do it, there must be blessing and divine illumination.

Mark, they did not seek Ezra's opinion, nor the ideas of Nehemiah, nor yet those of Zerubbabel. They honored these servants of God, and rightfully so; they would have despised the Master if they had not reverenced His sent ones; but the servants were to be ministers of the Word—

69

not of science or philosophy, nor yet of theology—but of the word of the living God; hence the cry, "Bring the Book!"

It is a grievous thing when merely human writings or words are put upon a level with the Book of books. One dreads the use often made of esteemed brethren's writings. Something is called in question, and at once there is a great effort made to show that Mr. So-and-So taught thus, or Mr. Somebody else has written this or the other. In this way the authority of the word of God is weakened in men's souls, and people are content if they think they hold what Mr. A. or Mr. B. held, even though they are quite unable to find authority for it in the book of God. This is a snare of which we need to be watchful lest we find ourselves once more teaching for doctrines the commandments of men.

Thirdly, we learn that when Ezra brought the book, "He read therein before the street that was before the Water Gate from the morning until midday, before the men and the women, and those that could understand; and the ears of all the people were attentive unto the book of the law" (ver. 3). This is most blessed—an attentive people solemnized by the word of God. So great was the company that a pulpit of wood was erected for Ezra, and on his right and left were companies of devoted Levites waiting to hear the Word and explain it to the people. It was a day when books were not easily multiplied. Perhaps Ezra had the only Bible there was in all the land; but in the manner indicated it was made the common property of all the people.

Subjection to the Word is the fourth point that comes prominently before us in verses 5 to 8. "Ezra opened the book in the sight of all the people (for he was above all the people); and when he opened it, all the people stood up: and Ezra blessed the Lord, the great God. And all the people answered, Amen, Amen, with lifting up their hands; and they bowed their heads, and worshipped the Lord with their faces to the ground." Who that has any conscience at all can fail to be touched by the reverence thus shown for the word of God? Such a Bible-reading was no free and easy, carnal coming together to argue over certain doctrines or debate intricate questions to the bewilderment of the simple, and the spiritual harm of the more advanced. Neither was it a place for some leader to shine, and to have his interpretations received without question as the mind of the Lord. This great Bible-reading was marked by a holy subjection to God and a hallowed reverence for His Word that contrasts strikingly with modern flippancy and irreverence in handling holy things.

To minister the Word to such a company must have been both a great joy and a solemn responsibility for Ezra and the Levites as they "caused the people to understand the law, and the people stood in their place. So they read in the book in the law of God distinctly, and gave the sense, and caused them to understand the reading" (vers. 7, 8). It needs to be borne in mind that, after the captivity, Hebrew, as a spoken language, had largely been displaced by Aramaic, hence the need of carefully explaining the Hebrew words to the waiting people.

Fifthly, the word of God as a source of joy and refreshment. This is what is suggested in the next section, verses 9 to 12: "And Nehemiah, that is the Tirshatha [or, governor], and Ezra the priest the scribe, and the Levites that taught the people, said unto all the people, This day is holy unto the Lord your God: mourn not, nor weep. For all the people wept when they heard the words of the law."

Their awakened consciences told them how guilty they and their fathers had been in refusing to obey the word of God; but their tears of penitence testified to the self-judgment that was going on; and, with God, sin judged is sin put away. Hence the cheering words of verse 10. "Then he said unto them, Go your way, eat the fat, and drink the sweet, and send portions unto them for whom nothing is prepared; for this day is holy unto our Lord: neither be ye sorry; for the joy of the Lord is your strength." God loves to surround Himself with a holy, happy people; but the two things of necessity go together. Holiness and happiness are inseparable. Who can fail to see in what is here before us a striking picture, often fulfilled, when God has visited His people in giving them bread? Refreshed and edified themselves, they become channels of blessing to others, sharing gladly with those "for whom nothing is prepared."

"So the Levites stilled all the people, saying, Hold your peace, for the day is holy, neither be ye grieved. And all the people went their way to eat and to drink, and to send portions, and to make great mirth, because they had understood the words that were declared unto them" (vers. 11, 12). How much deeper the joy to-day, in the light of a full gospel, when saints gather about a risen Christ, and His word is brought home to each heart in the Spirit's power, leading to similar exercises and lifting-up before God.

It is of *obedience* to the Word that the sixth section speaks. On the second day the chiefs of the people came together again, and the reading of the Word was continued. On this occasion a notable discovery was made: "They found written... that the children of Israel should dwell in booths in the feast of the seventh month" (ver. 14). Now this was at once recognized as a challenge to obedience. Here was something which had been *unobserved for a thousand years*—and still it was in the Book! Verse 17 shows us that in the palmiest days of David and Solomon no attention had been paid to this particular precept. "Since the days of Joshua the son of Nun unto that day had not the children of Israel done so." To obey it required considerable inconvenience; they might have argued that what Samuel, David, Solomon and others had overlooked was surely non-essential; but "they found it written," and that settled it for an obedient people. So the whole company went out to the mountains, and brought olive, pine, myrtle and palm branches and made booths, "as it is written," and in these they dwelt, thus calling to mind the days of God's care for His pilgrim people in the wilderness: "And there was very great gladness." What a lovely example of unquestioning obedience to the Word!

And so we come to the seventh thought, in closing our somewhat rapid survey of the chapter: The word of God is all-sufficient for every experience of life. "Also day by day, from the first day unto the last day, he read in the book of the law of God. And they kept the feast seven days; and on the eighth day was a solemn assembly, according to the manner" (ver. 18). Those seven days looked on to the Kingdom, when the Lord shall be surrounded by a happy, redeemed people, the *eighth* day bringing an outlook into eternity. Throughout Time the word of God contains all His people need for spiritual food and daily guidance.

Oh, for grace ever to hide that Word in our hearts, thus to be kept from sin, and to have our steps ordered accordingly, and every thought brought into captivity to the obedience of Christ!

Chapter IX The Word And Prayer

The relations of the word of God and prayer come out vividly in this portion. The seven days' ministry of the Word had had a most blessed effect so that "in the twenty and fourth day of this month (the same month that was ushered in by the great Bible-reading) the children of Israel were assembled with fasting, and with sack-clothes, and earth upon them. And the seed of Israel separated themselves from all strangers, and stood and confessed their sins, and the iniquities of their fathers. And they stood up in their place, and read in the book of the law of the Lord their God one fourth part of the day; and another fourth part they confessed, and worshiped the Lord their God" (vers. 1-3).

The order here is most instructive. It was *first* the Word, then prayer, confession, and worship. The Word had been having its effect in a wonderfully real way since the seven days' feast. What that Word judged, they had been judging. What that Word commanded they had sought to do. Hence we have as a result the remnant reaching what was probably the highest moral state they ever occupied from the Babylonian captivity to the coming of Messiah. Their separation was complete. "They separated themselves from *all* strangers." It was now for the first time that position and condition seemed to coalesce.

And so they come together again desiring to learn more of the mind of God that it might lead to increased devotedness. So the Bible-reading is again prominent. The first quarter of the day is spent in hearing the Word. Then the next quarter is given up to prayer: "They confessed and worshiped the Lord their God." It is unwise, and may be hurtful, to reverse this order. The Word and prayer should ever go together—but it should be the Word first;

then prayer follows intelligently. The believer should be a man holding the even balance of learning from the Word and cultivating the spirit of prayer. We need to hear God speaking to us that we may speak rightly to God.

One who gives himself pre-eminently to the Word, neglecting prayer, will become heady and doctrinal—likely to quarrel about "points," and be occupied with theoretical Christianity to the hurt of his soul and the irritation of his brethren. On the other hand, one who gives himself much to prayer while neglecting the Word is likely to become exceedingly introspective, mystical, and sometimes fanatical. But he who reads the word of God reverently and humbly, seeking to know the will of God, and then gives himself to prayer, confessing and judging what the Scriptures have condemned in his ways, and words, and thoughts, will have his soul drawn out in worship also, and thus grow both in grace and in knowledge, becoming a well-rounded follower of Christ. Apart from a knowledge of the Word, prayer will lack exceedingly in intelligence; for the objective must ever precede the subjective, but not be divorced therefrom.

Here, in Nehemiah 9 (which as we have elsewhere noticed is linked, in confession, with Daniel 9 and Ezra 9), the Levites lead the people in their prayer and praise, standing "on the stairs," as though going up to the heavenly sanctuary. And in the prayer that follows—the longest in the Bible (Solomon's dedicatory prayer being considerably shorter)—there is much blessed instruction as we listen to the rehearsal of God's ways with their fathers and the confession of their own failure and sin.

The opening words remind us of the beginning of what is generally called the Lord's prayer—and of what should occupy a pre-eminent place in *all prayer*—"Hallowed be

Thy Name." The Levites called on all the people to stand up and bless the Eternal One, their God, whose glorious name is exalted above all blessing and praise. To Him alone creation is ascribed and, as though testifying against the idolatry all about them that led the nations to worship and serve the creature rather than the Creator, they acknowledge that "all the host of heaven worship Him." He it was who had chosen Abram, bringing him out of the Chaldees, making him in very deed to answer to his new name Abraham—"the father of a multitude." To him the promise of the land of Canaan was given which in due course was fulfilled in his seed—multitudinous as the sand of the sea, brought out of Egyptian bondage, led through the sea and the wilderness by the cloudy pillar, first to the mount of God and then to the land of promise (vers. 4-12). The Levites celebrated the giving of the law at Sinai; and it is of moment to notice that they declare it was then—and not before—that the holy Sabbath was made known to them (ver. 14). This would seem conclusive evidence that whereas God sanctified the seventh day at the completion of His work, as recorded in the second chapter of Genesis, He did not give it to man by command until He had a redeemed people gathered about Himself in the wilderness. It was a sign, or reminder, not alone of God's rest after the creative days, but of the deliverance of Israel from Egyptian bondage, and the pledge of a rest yet to come.

After celebrating the mighty acts of the Lord, the Levites go on to confess the fearful breakdown of the people, and that from the very first. Their fathers dealt proudly, and in place of recognizing their dependence on this mighty Deliverer who had wrought so wondrously on their behalf, they hardened their necks and harkened not to His commandments—in their rebellion desiring even to return to the very land of bondage from which He had taken them. Their wilderness his- tory was a most humbling record, full of evidences of their folly, and yet abounding with testimonies of Jehovah's faithfulness, who sustained them through all those forty years "so that they lacked nothing; their clothes waxed not old, and their feet swelled not" (vers. 13-21). And when at last they reached the land given by covenant to Abraham, the nations therein were rooted out before them and they themselves planted in their place; there they multiplied and grew, rejoicing in the abundance of the fruitful fields of Canaan, and delighting themselves in the great goodness of their covenant-keeping God (vers. 22-25).

But disobedience and rebellion characterized them almost from the days of Joshua, and God's holy law they cast behind their back, despising His precepts and slaying His prophets, when such were sent to show them their sin and call them back to subjection to His word. When, in their distresses, they cried to Him He granted them deliverance—not for their deserts, but for His own name's sake, according to His mercies; thus again and again manifesting His tender love and care.

Yet scarcely had He interposed on their behalf than they turned aside as before, sinning against His judgments (that is, the testimonies rendered), "which if a man do he shall live in them," thus fighting against His Holy Spirit who spake in the prophets; until, at last, the kings of Assyria and Babylonia were permitted to root them out of their inheritance, carrying them captive to the land of the stranger.

The Levites own the justice of all God's dealings with the nation. "Thou hast done right, but we have done wickedly," is their humble acknowledgment. And they go on to confess how their kings, princes, priests and fathers had not kept the law, nor harkened to His commandments, nor turned from their wicked works; and so they remained bondmen to that very day, subject to the kings of Persia; even though a little reviving had been granted them, and they had been gathered once more at God's centre. Now, bearing in mind all the evil consequences of disobedience in the past, they made a "sure covenant" (alas, again to be soon broken!) and, putting it in writing, signed and sealed it; pledging themselves to cleave to the Lord, to separate from all strangers, and faithfully to do His will (vers. 33-38).

That they were truly in earnest none can doubt, but the future would show once more, as the past so often had done, that man is not to be trusted, and that were God's covenant based on human faithfulness, instead of divine grace, all hope for man's lasting blessing would be vain.

Yet it is well to have such seasons of exercise as this which we have been contemplating. Undoubtedly, it was for many a step forward, which they never retraced, although for the nation, as such, there could be no full restoration till the advent of God's Anointed.

Chapter X The New Start

It is both true and false (according to the thought one has in mind) that God never restores a failed testimony. If by this expression, frequently heard at the present time, it be meant that failure having once blighted a movement that originally was of God, it will never again reach its pristine glory, the statement is undoubtedly true. But if it be meant that, ruin having come in, God will not answer the cry of repentance with revival and restoration when His face is earnestly sought, it is utterly false. It is to be feared that it is spiritual lethargy and an unwillingness to bestir oneself and seriously face existing conditions, which are the real causes why many once gathered to the name of Jesus now go on in isolation, blaming the divisions and lack of spirituality evidenced by others as the reason for their having left the path of subjection to God's revealed will as to the corporate testimony of His people.

To such, what we have just been considering ought to speak loudly. Things had got indeed very low among the remnant. Their actual condition had become most dishonoring to God. Nevertheless their position was a right one, and nothing could be gained by forsaking it. The important thing was to remain where they were, and seek to put away all that hindered their enjoyment of the Lord's favor, that thus their state individually and corporately might be approved of Him.

So we have seen them turning unitedly to the Word, earnestly inquiring as to what God had said, and when "they found it written," acting upon it, though it meant, as in many instances it did, bitter sorrow and painful humiliation.

Having pledged themselves (in accord with the spirit of the legal dispensation) to put away all strangers and to walk obediently before God, they drew up a written declaration, signing and sealing it, from Nehemiah the Governor down to the lowest in rank of the common people, "all they that had separated themselves from the people of the lands unto the law of God, their wives, their sons, and their daughters, every one having knowledge, and having understanding" (vers. 1-28).

It was a serious, solemn and definite thing they had undertaken, and it would require purpose of heart to carry it out. "They clave to their brethren, their nobles, and entered into a curse, and into an oath, to walk in God's law, which was given by Moses the servant of God, and to observe and do all the commandments of Jehovah our Lord, and His judgments and His statutes; and that we would not give our daughters unto the peoples of the land, nor take their daughters for our sons: and if the peoples of the land bring ware or any victuals on the Sabbath day to sell, that we would not buy it of them on the Sabbath, or on the holy day: and that we would leave the seventh year, and the exaction of every debt" (vers. 29-31).

Notice carefully what it was they had covenanted to do—

First: To walk in God's law; or, in other words, to be subject to the Holy Scriptures. Second (and of course all that followed was involved in the first): To maintain separation from the peoples of the land that there be no unequal yoke. Third: To honor God by a careful observance of the Sabbath day, not permitting greed or lust for strangers' dainties to lead them to violate its sacredness. Fourth: To let the land lie fallow every seventh year, for disobedience to which command they had of old been carried to Babylon, while for seventy years the land kept Sabbath. Fifth: To deal graciously with each other as brethren, leaving the exaction of every debt, not acting in the spirit of the usurer.

Are there not weighty lessons for us in these pledges? I mean for those who have sought to give Christ His place as Head, and to act on the truth of the oneness of the body of Christ, but who have so miserably failed to keep the Spirit's unity in the bond of peace. Wherein have we missed our way? Has it not been in what is here set forth in Old Testament language? Must we not confess that we have not been obedient to the word of our God? We prided ourselves on having taken a right position—directed thereto by the Word—but we have not been careful to be individually subject to that Word. Is it not a fact that to many the "voice of the assembly" has been louder than the voice of God in Holy Scripture? Is it not a fact that the traditions of the elders have, in critical times, been more relied on than "Thus saith the Lord?" Is it not time then that, as individuals and as gathered companies of saints, we go back to the simplicity of early days, and seek to be guided henceforth alone by the word of the Lord which abideth forever?

And have we not, likewise, greatly missed the truth of separation? Have we not often been quite satisfied in that we were separated ecclesiastically from the world-church, while socially and in our business relations we were linked up with the world to an even greater extent than many not outwardly separated as we? Has not the spirit of the world come into our homes and assemblies? Is it not manifest in the books we enjoy, the clothing we wear, the company we frequent, the language we use? What is mere ecclesiastical separation if we are otherwise so much linked with the world?

And is it not true that, when we have been somewhat aroused as to this, we have enjoined strictest separation from saints often more godly than ourselves, instead of from the spirit of the present age of evil? Has it not often happened that saints of God have been passed by or coldly greeted because of some difference in judgment as to a disciplinary question difficult to determine righteously, while utter worldlings have been given every evidence of affection? These are serious questions that had better be faced now than at the judgment-seat of Christ.

We know that, as we are not under law but under grace, the Sabbath of a past dispensation is now for us fulfilled in Christ, but are we then giving Christ His place, and not permitting our greed for gain or our lust after earth's pleasant things to break in upon that Sabbath-rest we should ever enjoy in Him? Can our business affairs always bear the test of His eyes that are as a flame of fire? Have we one weight for testing sacred things and another for what we call secular affairs? May there not be cause for exercise as to these matters? And may it not be that right here is one reason for our leanness?

And what of the seventh year? It was this "leaving the seventh year" that really showed that Israel were a people confiding in the living God. "To live by faith" is often spoken of as though it were the calling or prerogative of those separated to the ministry of the Word. But are not *all* believers called to live by faith—to hold things here with a loose grasp, but lay hold on eternal life as the one thing needful? And have we been largely forgetting this, and contenting ourselves with "gathering on divine ground," "scripturally breaking bread," "maintaining the testimony," and all the rest of what is merely outward and ecclesiastical, while losing our grip on eternal realities and

82

living as though this world were by far the more important of the two? Is it any wonder then that when matters arise among us calling for the exercise of spiritual discernment and godly judgment we are found wanting, and what should be for the unifying of the saints becomes the means of their scattering?

And this brings us to the fifth pledge: What about the exaction of every debt? Have we not been hard and exacting and over-much righteous with one another, alienating those we ought to have drawn with cords of love, and demanding of each other what subjects of grace should be ashamed to press? Surely, as before intimated, it is high time to "leave off this usury."

The end of the dispensation is fast approaching. The Judge is standing at the door. The Lord is looking on, close at hand. The word of God is being given up and its truth denied on every hand. It is high time that those who love that Word cease their exactions one of another, and all alike judging everything that has hindered fellowship, put away for ever the evil things that have wrought such havoc, and so stand shoulder to shoulder, heart to heart, and hand in hand, for God and His truth with all who seek to be loyal to Him and His Word in the little time that remains ere "the coming of our Lord Jesus Christ and our gathering together unto Him."

On the rest of the chapter I have few remarks to offer. Judging the evil, the remnant sought, so far as they might, to put things in order in regard to providing for and maintaining the service of the house of God, giving of their first-fruits and tithes that there might be abundance to carry on the ministry and to support the ministers. Depend upon it, if the Lord's people get right individually, that which is corporate will flourish, and there will be abundant provision for maintaining a visible testimony. Lack of spirituality closes up hearts and purses. Godliness opens both. The poverty of the people was no barrier when their consciences were in exercise, and they determined "not to forsake the house of their God" (vers. 32-39). And so will it ever be where the love of Christ reigns.

Apart from this all must degenerate more and more until all testimony for God is gone. One who knew and suffered much as standing for "the present truth" left behind seasonable words of warning with which I bring this portion to a close.

"What is important is not 'The Brethren,' but the truth they have...God could set them aside, and spread His truth by others—would, I believe, though full of gracious patience, if they be not faithful. Their place is to remain in obscurity and devotedness, not to think of Brethren (it is always wrong to think of ourselves), but of souls, in Christ's name and love, and of His glory.

"Let them walk in love, in the truth, humble, as little (and content to be little) as when they began, and God will bless them. If not, their candlestick may go as that of others—and oh, what sorrow and confusion of face it would be after such grace!...

"As regards also the activity outside them, it is one of the signs of the times, and they should rejoice in it ... But it does not give their testimony at all... I do not believe attacks on anything to be our path. Self-defence is every way to be avoided. The Lord will answer for us if we do His will... God has no need of us, but He has need of a people who walk in the truth, in love, and holiness. 'I will leave in the midst of thee an afflicted and poor people, and they shall trust in the name of Jehovah' (Zeph. 3:12).

"The gospel we may, and must, rejoice in; yet it only makes the testimony of Brethren outside the camp more necessary than ever; but it must be real...If brethren fall in with the current Christianity inside the camp, they would be but another sect with certain truths"— *J.N. D.*

In the light of much that has transpired one can almost hear the voice of prophecy in such words. Beloved brethren, let us one and all heed their serious message.

Chapter XI A Willing People

The Bridegroom in the Canticles says: "I went down into the garden of nuts to see the fruits of the valley, and to see whether the vine flourished, and the pomegranates budded. Or ever I was aware, my soul set me among the chariots of my willing people" (Song 6:11, 12; 1911 *Version*); and in Psalm 110:3 we read, "Thy people shall be willing (or, a free-will offering) in the day of Thy power, in the beauties of holiness from the womb of the morning: thou hast the dew of thy youth."

Words like these form a fitting introduction to the chapter now soliciting our thoughtful consideration—a passage that seems to be filled only with hard names and meagre details if the important truth be passed over that it is God's own inspired honor-roll, never to be forgotten, of His willing people. Then indeed we recognize in it such a delightful valley as that described in the Song, where the vine is flourishing and the fragrant pomegranates budding for the delectation of Him who rejoices to dwell among His willing-hearted saints—made willing by His power working among them, manifested in holiness of heart and life, engendered and refreshed by the precious dews of the Holy Spirit.

A free-will offering was made, not now of money or other means, but of men devoted to the Lord, to dwell in Jerusalem, that the holy city might be furnished and defended. "And the rulers of the people dwelt at Jerusalem: the rest of the people also cast lots, to bring one of ten to dwell in Jerusalem the holy city, and nine parts to dwell in other cities. And the people blessed all the men that willingly offered themselves to dwell at Jerusalem" (vers. 1, 2). As before they had tithed their produce and possessions, so now they tithed themselves.

But it was not conscription; for each one chosen responded with a free heart, glad thus to be especially linked with the defence and upbuilding of the city of the Name. They loved the place where God's honor dwelt, and they were pleased to be at home there.

Of old, in the wilderness, it was the "willing-hearted and the wise-hearted" who built the sanctuary of the Lord; and may we not say that the willing-hearted *are* the wise-hearted? For surely it is the evidence of wisdom abiding in the heart when the whole life is freely devoted to the service of the Lord. And so when the evil had been put away from among the remnant of the Jews, and the interests of Jehovah had been made paramount to every other interest it was the free and loyal service of His willing people that gave joy to the heart of God.

To most of us, perhaps, the details that follow in the balance of the chapter can, in the very nature of things, possess very little interest. It is a mere tabulation of families and individuals whose names to us are often well-nigh unpronounceable, and usually, forgotten almost as soon as read. But in the sight of God it is a tabulation of great importance, and, like other lists we have noticed in these post-captivity books, will be consulted at the judgment-seat of Christ. For these willing offerers shall then learn how good was their choice when they accepted loss in this world that they might the better care for the city of God's choice. Very little is said of these members of the tribes of Judah and Benjamin (vers. 4-9), and of Levi also who dwelt in Jerusalem (vers. 10-18), but every one is well known to the Lord, and every word and act that told their devotedness of heart to Himself will be manifested in that day. And, even now, where scholarship enables one to read something of the significance of these names, there are doubtless helpful lessons which for the present most of us fail to see.

The porters and servants (the "Nethinim"), yea, and the singers too—true sons of Asaph set "over the business of the house of God" who had their special portion by the king's commandment (vers. 19-23)—will all be called by name when Messiah sits upon His throne to reward every one who in every dispensation had respect unto the coming recompense. For it was just as truly a service for some to till the fields and dwell in the restored villages, thus holding all the land for God, so far as strength and numbers permitted, as it was for their willing-hearted brethren to abide in the city of the coming King (vers. 25-36). He valued all according to the intention of the heart, and He does the same to-day.

We would not therefore pass carelessly over what some might call so "dry" a chapter as this, but reading it thoughtfully and prayerfully let us challenge our own hearts as to how far we have been and are now characterized by the spirit of willing, joyous obedience to all that God has been pleased to make known to us concerning His holy desires. Words need not be multiplied on such a theme; but exercise may well be real and deep, lest in that day, when the record of *our* service is opened on high, there be only a blotted story of slothful, almost forced obedience, contrasting unfavorably indeed with the willing offering of these men of old.

In view of this may we be stirred up to heed the Christian poet's words:

"Go on; go on; there's all eternity to rest in, And far too few are on the *active service list;* No labor for the Lord is risky to invest in; But nothing will make up should His 'Well done' be missed."

Chapter XII The Dedication Of The Wall

It will be remembered that in the duplicate lists of those who first came up to Jerusalem under Zerubbabel and Joshua the high priest (or Jeshua, as he is here called), the families only of the priests were mentioned, not the names of the chief priests themselves. That lack is supplied in the opening verses of the present chapter (vers. 1-7). God would have these men in everlasting remembrance, who so efficiently fulfilled their service with true-hearted devotion. The chief of the Levites are also mentioned, though of these we have read before in chapters 8:7 and 9:4, 5. A later generation of priests, serving doubtless in the latter days of Nehemiah, is given in verses 12 to 21, the sons of those referred to above, faithful men walking in their fathers' footsteps, and ensamples to the people.

But in the intervening verses (10 and 11) we have a short genealogical list carrying down the line of Jeshua for five generations to Jaddua, the great and justly-celebrated high priest who held this supreme office in the days when the Persian dominion was overthrown by Alexander the Great. There can, I think, be no question as to this table having been added by a later hand, which the Holy Spirit was pleased to use to preserve the record of Jaddua's descent. Verse 22 must have been added at the same time, declaring that a faithful record of the heads of the Levites had been kept to the days of Darius the Persian, whom I take to be Darius Codomanus, overthrown by the great Macedonian conqueror. It is possible indeed that the book of Malachi may have been written about that time, and that he may have added to the list, or the list itself. His solemn message shows us the sad condition into which the children of the remnant degenerated after the fathers had died.

Simple souls will not be confused or perplexed at the suggestion we have made above, if they bear in mind that the entire Old Testament was in the hands of the Jewish doctors in the days of our Lord's sojourn upon earth, and that concerning it all He declared, "The Scripture cannot be broken." It is not necessary therefore to know in each instance the human author of a book or part of a book. We know that "holy men of God spake as they were moved by the Holy Ghost and thus we have in every part a "God-breathed" record, and that is enough.

It is evident from the next table (vers. 23-26) that both Nehemiah and Ezra lived through "the days of Joiakim the son of Jeshua," as well as in the days of the father, who accompanied Zerubbabel in.the first emigration from Babylon. Dur- ing their life-time the people clung to the word of God, and, with occasional individual lapses, such as we read of in the next chapter, maintained, on the whole, a testimony for the Lord who had brought them back, though in feebleness, to the place where He had set His name. Of the chief of the Levites (ver. 24) it is distinctly said that they were appointed both "to praise and to give thanks, according to the commandment of David the man of God, ward over against ward." The temple might be poor indeed as compared with Solomon's building, "exceeding magnifical," and the people themselves a small and afflicted remnant, but they sought to act on the divine instruction as to the service of the house of God which had been communicated by David to Solomon at the beginning. Likewise, whatever the feebleness to-day, it is the part of faithfulness to go back to "that which was from the beginning," and to endeavor, though in weakness, to carry out that which is written in the word of God.

The present chapter is divided into two almost equal parts, the first twenty-six verses belonging properly to chapter eleven, as being entirely composed of genealogical tables similar to those of the previous chapter. The second division continues the course of the history, and contains the account of the feast of the dedication of the now completed wall of Jerusalem. This was turned into a great occasion of rejoicing and thanksgiving to God, who had not only brought the people back from the strangers' land but had permitted them to surround His house and His holy city with a separating wall, testifying both to friends and enemies alike that they were under His care who had once scattered their nation because of unjudged sin.

From every quarter the Levites gathered "to keep the dedication with gladness, both with thanksgivings, and with singing, with cymbals, psalteries, and with harps" (ver. 27). It was a gladsome occasion indeed, and worthy of being joyously commemorated in coming years.

"The sons of the singers" were gathered together all about the city to participate in the general rejoicing. Jerusalem's wall was a symbol of salvation and her gates of praise.

After the priests and Levites had concluded a ceremony of purification, dedicating the people, the gates, and the wall to the Lord, Nehemiah brought up the princes of Judah upon the wall and divided all into two great companies, stretching out on the right and the left "toward the Dung Gate." With trumpets pealing out their notes of gladness and voices lifted up in songs of praise, the Levites and priests answered one another in antiphonal chants, after the manner of the 24th psalm, Nehemiah leading one company and Ezra the scribe the other. Thank-offerings were offered upon the altar, and "God made them rejoice with great joy"—as He always does when His people walk before Him in holiness and truth (vers. 31-43).

Nor were the servants of the Lord forgotten, for the people brought their tithes into the storehouse, and out of willing hearts gave abundantly for the maintenance of the sons of Aaron, in accordance with the Word (vers. 44-47).

One is reminded of the two-fold offering of Heb. 13:15,16: "By Him therefore let us offer the sacrifice of praise to God continually, that is, the fruit of our lips, giving thanks to His name. But to do good and to communicate, forget not: for with such sacrifices God is well pleased." These two offerings should never be divorced—thanksgiving going up to God from grateful hearts, and benevolence flowing forth toward men, the practical expression of that gratitude.

There is no surer indication of a low state in God's people than to find the poor among them left to suffer want, and the Lord's servants permitted to endure privation. These last are called to a path of trial, and must needs learn to be abased as well as to abound, to be full and to be empty; but whatever blessing they may find as they thus share Christ's sufferings, it is to the shame of the people of God, whose debtors they are. Were there more conscientious concern about this matter in many places, there would be richer and fuller ministry vouchsafed by God to His people, and more blessing in the assemblies of His saints, who often need to be reminded that:

"It never was loving that emptied a heart, Nor giving that emptied a purse."

Let God be honored with the first-fruits of our substance, and He will soon prove that He will be no man's debtor, but will abundantly confirm the word spoken by Malachi the prophet: "Bring ye all the tithes into the storehouse, that there may be meat in my house, and prove Me now herewith, saith the Lord of hosts, if I will not open you the windows of heaven, and pour you out a blessing that there shall not be room enough to receive it. And I will rebuke the devourer for your sakes, and he shall not destroy the fruits of your ground; neither shall your vine cast her fruit before the time in the field, saith the Lord of hosts" (Mal. 3:10, 11). That this illustrates a great spiritual truth is certain. That many have proven it to be intensely literal is equally sure. And it has been to the eternal loss of greater numbers who have failed in this very thing, and forgotten that they were only the stewards, not the owners, of wealth entrusted to them, to be used in view of the everlasting habitations.

Chapter XIII Vigilance *Versus* Declension

The striking contrast between the praiseworthy vigilance of Nehemiah in detecting and dealing with various phases of declension, and the continual tendency to drift away from obedience to the written Word, on the part of many of the people, is most marked in this closing chapter.

That serious evils soon developed is well known to the student of Jewish history. These were of two characters. On the one hand the separation truth of Nehemiah's day was soon held in a onesided manner, so that position was everything and condition quite ignored. This resulted in Pharisaism—doctrinally correct in the main, but cold, rigid, and heartless—glorying in separation while ignoring the weightier matters of true piety and godly benevolence. On the other hand there was a re-action against all that savored of the puritanism of those days, so that the mass of the people became careless and indifferent, and, save that idolatry was never reinstated, became as impious as their fathers whose sins had brought the captivity. In all this we may well read a solemn warning, bidding us never separate condition from position, nor piety toward God from grace toward needy men.

Sanctification in its practical aspect is by the truth. Hence it is ever gradual—as the truth is learned in the fear of God. Of this we have a splendid example in the first nine verses. On the very day of the dedication of the wall (for so I understand the opening phrase), that portion of the book of Deuteronomy (chap. 23:3, 4) was read, which we have already quoted in our notes on chapter two, and which commanded that the Ammonite and the Moabite should be excluded from the congregation of the Lord forever because of their iniquitous course towards Israel in the wilderness. This at once led to a closer application of the truth of separation than before. They had previously separated from all strangers; now they "separated from Israel all the mixed multitude" (ver. 3).

Of Tobiah the Ammonite, who had so bitterly resented the building of the wall in the beginning, and whose wiles had failed to turn Nehemiah aside from his purpose, we have not heard for a long time. Now we get the startling information that Eliashib the priest, who had the oversight of the dwellings of the priests at the house of God, had made a secret alliance with Tobiah during a hitherto unnoticed absence of Nehemiah, in which time he had returned to wait upon the king. The vigilant governor's eye being no longer upon him, Eliashib abused his liberty by preparing "a great chamber" for the ungodly Ammonite, which had been formerly used as a storehouse for the tithes and offerings. Probably this apartment was never occupied by Tobiah, for, ere Eliashib's plan could be fully carried out, Nehemiah returned. Hearing "of the evil that Eliashib did for Tobiah in preparing him a chamber in the courts of the house of God," he was sorely grieved, but acted with his accustomed energy, thwarting the unholy purpose by casting the stuff of Tobiah out of the room and cleansing the chambers, into which he again brought the hallowed vessels with the offerings. What an example for the people; nor do we again read of any effort on the part of Tobiah to get a foothold in Jerusalem.

But another evil soon claimed the returned governor's attention. God's servants were being neglected by a self-seeking people, and unable to support those dependent upon them, the Levites and the singers, who a little before had willingly offered themselves for the service of the house of God, had gone back to their fields, toiling for daily bread. The test, doubtless, revealed a weakness in these men themselves, but it also showed the declining state of the people in neglecting the temporalities of the house of the Lord; so Nehemiah contends with the rulers, and stirs them up to attend to the gathering of the unpaid tithes. This being accomplished, the Levites could attend on their service (vers. 10-14).

A third sign of declension, encroaching upon the former determination to be faithful to God, was evidenced in the laxity of some as to the sanctity of the Sabbath, the Lord's holy day, concerning which there had been such particular pledges made. Nehemiah saw some treading winepresses and engaged in other secular occupations on the Sabbath, even buying and selling and carrying burdens on the day of rest. In vain at first he testified against them. Strangers from Tyre brought fish and other kinds of produce which they offered for sale, and for which they found ready buyers on the Sabbath. Thoroughly aroused, Nehemiah contended with the nobles, the rulers of the people, charging this profanation of the holy day upon them, and reminding them that it was for sin such as this that all the past evil had befallen the Jews and the city of Jerusalem. "Yet," he cries, indignantly, "ye bring more wrath upon Israel by profaning the Sabbath" (vers. 13-18).

So, with his accustomed energy, he commanded the gates to be shut at sundown, as the Sabbath drew on, and not to be opened till it was past, while guards were set to see that no burden of any kind was brought into the city on that day. Once or twice the merchants and hucksters lodged all night and all day outside Jerusalem, vainly pleading for admission, but Nehemiah's orders were carried out to the letter. Finally, he threatened them with arrest if they came again with their wares on the Sabbath.

Seeing the orders were meant to be carried out, they came no more on that day.

As polluted, the Levites were then commanded to cleanse themselves, and henceforth maintain a guard over the gates "to sanctify the Sabbath day." Thus for the time the evil was again judged and the declension stayed (vers. 17-22).

But not yet could vigilance be relaxed. The flesh was still at work. In spite of all that they had heard and seen, some had been marrying women of Ashdod, Ammon and Moab. They may have excused themselves, as many do now, on the plea that they might lead these women to know and worship the one true God and learn the ways of Israel. But it was all a delusion. Children had been born of these unions, and these children were witness to the corruption that had been brought in. They "spake half in the speech of Ashdod, and could not speak in the Jews' language, but according to the language of each people" (vers. 23, 24). This is ever the fruit of such a yoke in marriage. The children soon follow the ways of the unregenerate parent and use the language of the flesh. Too late is the error realized. Too readily they follow the example and speech of the parent who knows not God.

Again Nehemiah's righteous anger burst forth. He contended with these unfaithful Jews and invoked the solemn judgments of the law upon them, even smiting some, and demanded of all that they swear by God no longer to countenance in any way these mixed marriages, from which only evil fruit could come. He reminded them how Solomon himself had failed so miserably because of this very thing, and besought them to harken unto the law and not expect others to condone their offences (vers. 25-27). No doubt some would speak of his ways as hard and bitter; but *sin* is hard and bitter; and persistency in it often requires severe measures to put things right. It is often not a sign of spirituality to be placid and sentimentally affectionate. Such behavior frequently tells of a conscience asleep and a soul unexercised. There was a time when the Lord Jesus made a scourge of small cords—a bitter whip—to drive out the trader? from God's house (John 2:15). Paul's language too was cutting and denunciatory when Satan's emissaries were seeking to overthrow divine truth; and God's wrath too shall be poured out without mixture in the cup of His indignation.

Another instance of declension closes both the chapter and the book. The grandson of Eliashib, the high priest, having married a daughter of Sanballat, the man of God, Nehemiah, drives him away from his presence. His grandfather's failure is brought again to mind in the descendant's defection.[7] Remembering Eliashib's intriguing with Tobiah, we are not surprised to read of his grandson's association with the family of Sanballat. In defiance of all that Nehemiah had been insisting on, this youth had married the guileful Horonite's daughter. He was the last with whom the governor had to deal, and he graphically declares, "Therefore I chased him from me." We can almost see the indignant countenance of the now aged Nehemiah as he learns of the perfidious-ness of the son of Joiada, and we cannot but admire the energy with which the doughty old warrior drives the culprit from his presence—even making intercession in the spirit of Elijah *against* those who had defiled the priesthood and violated the covenant. Only by such stern measures could they be cleansed from all strangers.

Consistent to the last, Nehemiah appointed "the wards of the priests and the Levites, every one in his business; and for the wood-offering, at times appointed, and for the first-fruits." Nothing was too great for his faith, and nothing was too insignificant for his consideration if it concerned the house, the people, or the honor of the Lord his God. This was indeed "a faithful man, and one that feared God above many"—just such an one as the times demanded, and he held on his way unflinchingly to the end, neither cajoled by flattery nor intimidated by opposition, for to him the approbation of the God of Israel was infinitely more than the good opinion of carnal or natural men.

And so with the prayer, "Remember me, O my God, for good!" the record comes to an abrupt termination, and Nehemiah passes from our view, only to appear again at the manifestation of the sons of God.

If we would learn something of the after-state of the Jew's we must turn, as previously intimated, to the last book of the Old Testament, where we learn through Malachi's stern charges the low state into which the remnant had fallen; while the Gospels and the Acts give us the solemn sequel and show the children of those returned from the captivity rejecting both the Son of God come in flesh to them, and the Holy Spirit also!

Well will it be for Christians who may read these lines, to lay all to heart, that similar declension may be through the mercy of God averted in the present age of grace. May He grant it for His name's sake and the glory of His beloved Son. Amen!

[1] Extracted from a letter by P. J. Loizeaux.

[2] See "Notes on the Book of Ezra," by the same.

[3] Archibald Brown, of London.

[4] The verse is really an exclamatory rather than a declarative sentence: "Remember Jesus Christ, of the seed of David, raised from the dead according to my gospel!"

[5] This little word "so" is quite characteristic of Nehemiah. It is found about twenty times.

[6] Those who are accustomed to the "Little Flock Hymn Book" might see in No. 235 a typical psalm; in No. 150, an almost matchless hymn; while No. 139 is a good example of a spiritual song.

[7] It is not certain, though probable, that Eliashib the high priest is the same as Eliashib the chief priest of verse 4.

Made in the USA
Middletown, DE
08 August 2023